Christianity as My
and the Mysteries of Antiquity

Rudolf Steiner

Alpha Editions

This edition published in 2024

ISBN : 9789367243251

Design and Setting By
Alpha Editions
www.alphaedis.com
Email - info@alphaedis.com

As per information held with us this book is in Public Domain.
This book is a reproduction of an important historical work. Alpha Editions uses the best technology to reproduce historical work in the same manner it was first published to preserve its original nature. Any marks or number seen are left intentionally to preserve its true form.

Contents

PREFACE TO THE SECOND EDITION ....- 1 -
I ....- 4 -
II ....- 8 -
III ....- 19 -
IV ....- 28 -
V ....- 39 -
VI ....- 52 -
VII ....- 60 -
VIII ....- 65 -
IX ....- 72 -
X ....- 80 -
XI ....- 82 -
XII ....- 87 -
XIII ....- 92 -
NOTES ....- 96 -

PREFACE TO THE SECOND EDITION

Christianity as Mystical Fact was the title given by the author to this work, when, eight years ago, he gathered into it the substance of lectures delivered by him in 1902. The title indicated the special character of the book. In it the attempt was made, not merely to represent historically the mystical content of Christianity, but to describe the origin of Christianity from the standpoint of mystical contemplation. Underlying this intention was the thought that at the genesis of Christianity mystical facts were at work which can only be perceived by such contemplation.

It is only the book itself which can make clear that by "mystical" its author does not imply a conception which relies more on vague feelings than on "strictly scientific statements." It is true that "mysticism" is at present widely understood in the former sense, and hence it is declared by many to be a sphere of the human soul-life with which "true science" can have nothing to do. In this book the word "mysticism" is used in the sense of the representation of a spiritual fact, which can only be recognised in its true nature when the knowledge of it is derived from the sources of spiritual life itself. If the kind of knowledge drawn from such sources is rejected, the reader will not be in a position to judge of the contents of this book. Only one who allows that the same clearness may exist in mysticism as in a true representation of the facts of natural science, will be ready to admit that the content of Christianity as mysticism may also be mystically described. For it is not only a question of the contents of the book, but first and foremost of the methods of knowledge by means of which the statements in it are made.

Many there are in the present day who have a most violent dislike to such methods, which are regarded as conflicting with the ways of true science. And this is not only the case with those willing to admit other interpretations of the world than their own, on the ground of "genuine knowledge of natural science," but also with those who as believers wish to study the nature of Christianity.

The author of this book stands on the ground of a conception which sees that the achievements of natural science in our age must lead up into true mysticism. In fact, any other attitude as regards knowledge actually contradicts everything presented by the achievements of natural science. The facts of natural science itself indeed cannot be comprehended by means of those methods of knowledge which so many people would like to employ to the exclusion of others, under the illusion that they stand on the firm ground of natural science. It is only when we are prepared to admit that a full appreciation of our present admirable knowledge of nature is compatible with genuine mysticism, that we can take the contents of this book into consideration.

The author's intention is to show, by means of what is here called "mystical knowledge," how the source of Christianity prepared its own ground in the mysteries of pre-Christian times. In this pre-Christian mysticism we find the soil in which Christianity throve, as a germ of quite independent nature. This point of view makes it possible to understand Christianity in its independent being, even though its evolution is traced from pre-Christian mysticism. If this point of view be overlooked, it is very possible to misunderstand that independent character, and to think that Christianity was merely a further development of what already existed in pre-Christian mysticism. Many people of the present day have fallen into this error, comparing the content of Christianity with pre-Christian conceptions, and then thinking that Christian ideas were only a continuation of the former. The following pages are intended to show that Christianity presupposes the earlier mysticism just as a seed must have its soil. It is intended to emphasise the peculiar character of the essence of Christianity, through the knowledge of its evolution, but not to extinguish it.

It is with deep satisfaction that the author is able to mention that this account of the nature of Christianity has found acceptance with a writer who has enriched the culture of our time in the highest sense of the word, by his important works on the spiritual life of humanity. Edouard Schuré, author of *Les Grands Initiés*,[1] is so far in accord with the attitude of this book that he undertook to translate it into French, under the title, *Le mystère chrétien et les mystères antiques*. It may be mentioned by the way, and as a symptom of the existence at the present time of a longing to understand the nature of Christianity as presented in this work, that the first edition was translated into other European languages besides French.

The author has not found occasion to alter anything essential in the preparation of this second edition. On the other hand, what was written eight years ago has been enlarged, and the endeavour has been made to express many things more exactly and circumstantially than was then possible. Unfortunately the author was obliged, through stress of work, to let a long period elapse between the time when the first edition was exhausted, and the appearance of the second.

Rudolf Steiner.

May, 1910.

FOOTNOTES:

[1] This book is to be had in an English translation, by F. Rothwell, under the title of *The Great Initiates*, A Sketch of the Secret History of Religions, by Edouard Schuré (Pub., Rider & Son, London).

I

POINTS OF VIEW

Natural Science has deeply influenced modern thought. It is becoming more and more impossible to speak of spiritual needs and the life of the soul, without taking into consideration the achievements and methods of this science. It must be admitted, however, that many people satisfy these needs, without letting themselves be troubled by its influence. But those who feel the beating of the pulse of the age must take this influence into consideration. With increasing swiftness do ideas derived from natural science take possession of our brains, and, unwillingly though it may be, our hearts follow, often in dejection and dismay. It is not a question only of the number thus won over, but of the fact that there is a force within the method of natural science, which convinces the attentive observer that that method contains something which cannot be neglected, and is one by which any modern conception of the universe must be profoundly affected. Many of the outgrowths of this method compel a justifiable rejection. But such rejection is not sufficient in an age in which very many resort to this way of thinking, and are attracted to it as if by magic. The case is in no way altered because some people see that true science long ago passed, by its own initiative, beyond the shallow doctrines of force and matter taught by materialists. It would be better, apparently, to listen to those who boldly declare that the ideas of natural science will form the basis of a new religion. If these ideas also appear shallow and superficial to one who knows the deeper spiritual needs of humanity, he must nevertheless take note of them, for it is to them that attention is now turned, and there is reason to think they will claim more and more notice in the near future.

Another class of people have also to be taken into account, those whose hearts have lagged behind their heads. With their reason they cannot but accept the ideas of natural science. The burden of proof is too much for them. But those ideas cannot satisfy the religious needs of their souls,—the perspective offered is too dreary. Is the human soul to rise on the wings of enthusiasm to the heights of beauty, truth, and goodness, only for each individual to be swept away in the end like a bubble blown by the material brain? This is a feeling which oppresses many minds like a nightmare. But scientific concepts oppress them also, coming as they do come with the mighty force of authority. As long as they can, these people remain blind to the discord in their souls. Indeed they console themselves by saying that full clearness in these matters is denied to the human soul. They think in accordance with natural science so long as the experience of their senses and the logic of their intellect demand it, but they keep to the religious sentiments in which they have been educated, and prefer to remain in darkness as to these matters,—a darkness which clouds their understanding. They have not the courage to battle through to the light.

There can be no doubt whatever that the habit of thought derived from natural science is the greatest force in modern intellectual life, and it must not be passed by heedlessly by any one concerned with the spiritual interests of humanity. But it is none the less true that the way in which it sets about satisfying spiritual needs is superficial and shallow. If this were the right way, the outlook would indeed be dreary. Would it not be depressing to be obliged to agree with those who say: "Thought is a form of force. We walk by means of the same force by which we think. Man is an organism which transforms various forms of force into thought-force, an organism the activity of which we maintain by what we call 'food,' and with which we produce what we call 'thought.' What a marvellous chemical process it is which could change a certain quantity of food into the divine tragedy of Hamlet." This is quoted from a pamphlet of Robert G. Ingersoll, bearing the title, *Modern Twilight of the Gods*. It matters little if such thoughts find but scanty acceptance in the outside world. The point is that innumerable people find themselves compelled by the system of natural science to take up with regard to world-processes an attitude in conformity with the above, even when they think they are not doing so.

It would certainly be a dreary outlook if natural science itself compelled us to accept the creed proclaimed by many of its modern prophets. Most dreary of all for one who has gained, from the content of natural science, the conviction that in its own sphere its mode of thought holds good and its methods are unassailable. For he is driven to make the admission that, however much people may dispute about individual questions, though volume after volume may be written, and thousands of observations accumulated about the struggle for existence and its insignificance, about the omnipotence or powerlessness of natural selection, natural science itself is moving in a direction which, within certain limits, must find acceptance in an ever-increasing degree.

But are the demands made by natural science really such as they are described by some of its representatives? That they are not so is proved by the method employed by these representatives themselves. The method they use in their own sphere is not such as is often described, and claimed for other spheres of thought. Would Darwin and Ernst Haeckel ever have made their great discoveries about the evolution of life if, instead of observing life and the structure of living beings, they had shut themselves up in a laboratory and there made chemical experiments with tissue cut out of an organism? Would Lyell have been able to describe the development of the crust of the earth if, instead of examining strata and their contents, he had scrutinised the chemical qualities of innumerable rocks? Let us really follow in the footsteps of these investigators who tower like giants in the domain of modern science. We shall then apply to the higher regions of spiritual life the methods they have used in the study of nature. We shall not then believe we have understood the nature of the "divine" tragedy of Hamlet by saying that a wonderful chemical process transformed a certain quantity of food into that tragedy. We shall believe it as little as an investigator of nature could seriously believe that he has understood the mission of heat in the evolution of the earth, when he has studied the action of heat on sulphur in a retort. Neither does he attempt to understand the construction of the human brain by examining the effect of liquid potash on a fragment of it, but rather by inquiring how the brain has, in the course of evolution, been developed out of the organs of lower organisms.

It is therefore quite true that one who is investigating the nature of spirit can do nothing better than learn from natural science. He need only do as science does, but he must not allow himself to be misled by what individual representatives of natural science would dictate to him. He must investigate in the spiritual as they do in the physical domain, but he need not adopt the opinions they entertain about the spiritual world, confused as they are by their exclusive contemplation of physical phenomena.

We shall only be acting in the spirit of natural science if we study the spiritual development of man as impartially as the naturalist observes the sense-world. We shall then certainly be led, in the domain of spiritual life, to a kind of contemplation which differs from that of the naturalist as geology differs from pure physics and biology from chemistry. We shall be led up to higher methods, which cannot, it is true, be those of natural science, though quite conformable with the spirit of it. Such methods alone are able to bring us to the heart of spiritual developments, such as that of Christianity, or other worlds of religious conceptions. Any one applying these methods may arouse the opposition of many who believe they are thinking scientifically, but he will know himself, for all that, to be in full accord with a genuinely scientific method of thought.

An investigator of this kind must also go beyond a merely historical examination of the documents relating to spiritual life. This is necessary just on account of the attitude he has acquired from his study of natural history. When a chemical law is explained, it is of small use to describe the retorts, dishes, and pincers which have led to the discovery of the law. And it is just as useless, when explaining the origin of Christianity, to ascertain the historical sources drawn upon by the Evangelist St. Luke, or those from which the "hidden revelation" of St. John is compiled. History can in this case be only the outer court to research proper. It is not by tracing the historical origin of documents that we shall discover anything about the dominant ideas in the writings of Moses or in the traditions of the Greek mystics. These documents are only the outer expression for the ideas. Nor does the naturalist who is investigating the nature of man trouble about the origin of the word "man," or the way in which it has developed in a language. He keeps to the thing, not to the word in which it finds expression. And in studying spiritual life we must likewise abide by the spirit and not by outer documents.

II

THE MYSTERIES AND THEIR WISDOM

A kind of mysterious veil hangs over the manner in which spiritual needs were satisfied during the older civilisations by those who sought a deeper religious life and fuller knowledge than the popular religions offered. If we inquire how these needs were satisfied, we find ourselves led into the dim twilight of the mysteries, and the individual seeking them disappears for a time from our observation. We see how it is that the popular religions cannot give him what his heart desires. He acknowledges the existence of the gods, but knows that the ordinary ideas about them do not solve the great problems of existence. He seeks a wisdom which is jealously guarded by a community of priest-sages. His aspiring soul seeks a refuge in this community. If he is found by the sages to be sufficiently prepared, he is led up by them, step by step, to higher knowledge, in places hidden from the eyes of outward observers. What then happens to him is concealed from the uninitiated. He seems for a time to be entirely removed from earthly life and to be transported into a hidden world.

When he reappears in the light of day a different, quite transformed person is before us. We see a man who cannot find words sublime enough to express the momentous experience through which he has passed. Not merely metaphorically but in a most real sense does he seem to have gone through the gate of death and to have awakened to a new and higher life. He is, moreover, quite certain that no one who has not had a similar experience can understand his words.

This was what happened to those who were initiated into the Mysteries, into that secret wisdom withheld from the people and which threw light on the greatest questions. This "secret" religion of the elect existed side by side with the popular religion. Its origin vanishes, as far as history is concerned, into the obscurity in which the origin of nations is lost. We find this secret religion everywhere amongst the ancients as far as we know anything concerning them; and we hear their sages speak of the Mysteries with the greatest reverence. What was it that was concealed in them? And what did they unveil to the initiate?

The enigma becomes still more puzzling when we discover that the ancients looked upon the Mysteries as something dangerous. The way leading to the secrets of existence passed through a world of terrors, and woe to him who tried to gain them unworthily. There was no greater crime than the "betrayal" of secrets to the uninitiated. The "traitor" was punished with death and the confiscation of his property. We know that the poet Æschylus was accused of having reproduced on the stage something from the Mysteries. He was only able to escape death by fleeing to the altar of Dionysos and by legally proving that he had never been initiated.

What the ancients say about these secrets is significant, but at the same time ambiguous. The initiate is convinced that it would be a sin to tell what he knows and also that it would be sinful for the uninitiated to listen. Plutarch speaks of the terror of those about to be initiated, and compares their state of mind to preparation for death. A special mode of life had to precede initiation, tending to give the spirit the mastery over the senses. Fasting, solitude, mortifications, and certain exercises for the soul were the means employed. The things to which man clings in ordinary life were to lose all their value for him. The whole trend of his life of sensation and feeling was to be changed.

There can be no doubt as to the meaning of such exercises and tests. The wisdom which was to be offered to the candidate for initiation could only produce the right effect upon his soul if he had previously purified the lower life of his sensibility. He was introduced to the life of the spirit. He was to behold a higher world, but he could not enter into relations with that world without previous exercises and tests. The relations thus gained were the condition of initiation.

In order to obtain a correct idea on this matter, it is necessary to gain experience of the intimate facts of the growth of knowledge. We must feel that there are two widely divergent attitudes towards that which the highest knowledge gives. The world surrounding us is to us at first the real one. We feel, hear, and see what goes on in it, and because we thus perceive things with our senses, we call them real. And we reflect about events, in order to get an insight into their connections. On the other hand, what wells up in our soul is at first not real to us in the same sense. It is "merely" thoughts and ideas. At the most we see in them only images of reality. They themselves have no reality, for we cannot touch, see, or hear them.

There is another way of being connected with things. A person who clings to the kind of reality described above will hardly understand it, but it comes to certain people at some moment in their lives. To them the whole connection with the world is completely reversed. They then call the images which well up in the spiritual life of their souls actually real, and they assign only a lower kind of reality to what the senses hear, touch, feel, and see. They know that they cannot prove what they say, that they can only relate their new experiences, and that when relating them to others they are in the position of a man who can see and who imparts his visual impressions to one born blind. They venture to impart their inner experiences, trusting that there are others round them whose spiritual eyes, though as yet closed, may be opened by the power of what they hear. For they have faith in humanity and want to give it spiritual sight. They can only lay before it the fruits which their spirit has gathered. Whether another sees them, depends on his spiritual eyes being opened or not.

There is something in man which at first prevents him from seeing with the eyes of the spirit. He is not there for that purpose. He is what his senses are, and his intellect is only the interpreter and judge of them. The senses would ill fulfil their mission if they did not insist upon the truth and infallibility of their evidence. An eye must, from its own point of view, uphold the absolute reality of its perceptions. The eye is right as far as it goes, and is not deprived of its due by the eye of the spirit. The latter only allows us to see the things of sense in a higher light. Nothing seen by the eye of sense is denied, but a new brightness, hitherto unseen, radiates from what is seen. And then we know that what we first saw was only a lower reality. We see that still, but it is immersed in something higher, which is spirit. It is now a question of whether we realise and feel what we see. One who lives only in the sensations and feelings of the senses will look upon impressions of higher things as a Fata Morgana, or mere play of fancy. His feelings are entirely directed towards the things of sense. He grasps emptiness when he tries to lay hold of spirit forms. They withdraw from him when he gropes after them. They are just "mere" thoughts. He thinks them, but does not live in them. They are images, less real to him than fleeting dreams. They rise up like bubbles while he is standing in his reality; they disappear before the massive, solidly built reality of which his senses tell him.

It is otherwise with one whose perceptions and feelings with regard to reality have changed. For him that reality has lost its absolute stability and value. His senses and feelings need not become numbed, but they begin to be doubtful of their absolute authority. They leave room for something else. The world of the spirit begins to animate the space left.

At this point a possibility comes in which may prove terrible. A man may lose his sensations and feelings of outer reality without finding any new reality opening up before him. He then feels himself as if suspended in the void. He feels as if he were dead. The old values have disappeared and no new ones have arisen in their place. The world and man no longer exist for him. This, however, is by no means a mere possibility. It happens at some time or other to every one who is seeking for higher knowledge. He comes to a point at which the spirit represents all life to him as death. He is then no longer in the world, but under it,—in the nether world. He is passing through Hades. Well for him if he sink not! Happy if a new world open up before him! Either he dwindles away or he appears to himself transfigured. In the latter case he beholds a new sun and a new earth. The whole world has been born again for him out of spiritual fire.

It is thus that the initiates describe the effect of the Mysteries upon them. Menippus relates that he journeyed to Babylon in order to be taken to Hades and to be brought back again by the successors of Zarathustra. He says that he swam across the great water on his wanderings, and that he passed through fire and ice. We hear that the Mystics were terrified by a flashing sword, and that blood flowed. We understand this when we know from experience the point of transition from lower to higher knowledge. We then feel as if all solid matter and things of sense had dissolved into water, and as if the ground were cut away from under our feet. Everything is dead which we felt before to be alive. The spirit has passed through the life of the senses, as a sword pierces a warm body; we have seen the blood of sense-nature flow. But a new life has appeared. We have risen from the nether-world. The orator Aristides relates this: "I thought I touched the god and felt him draw near, and I was then between waking and sleeping. My spirit was so light that no one who is not initiated can speak of or understand it." This new existence is not subject to the laws of lower life. Growth and decay no longer affect it. One may say much about the Eternal, but words of one who has not been through Hades are "mere sound and smoke." The initiates have a new conception of life and death. Now for the first time do they feel they have the right to speak about immortality. They know that one who speaks of it without having been initiated talks of something which he does not understand. The uninitiated attribute immortality only to something which is subject to the laws of growth and decay. The Mystics, however, did not merely desire to gain the conviction that the kernel of life is eternal. According to the view of the Mysteries, such a conviction would be quite valueless, for this view holds that the Eternal is not present as a living reality in the uninitiated. If such an one spoke of the Eternal, he would be speaking of something non-existent. It is rather the Eternal itself that the Mystics are seeking. They have first to awaken the Eternal within them, then they can speak of it. Hence the hard saying of Plato is quite real to them, that the uninitiated sinks into the mire, and that only one who has passed through the mystical life enters eternity. It is only in this sense that the words in the fragment of Sophocles can be understood: "Thrice-blessed are the initiated who come to the realm of the shades. They alone have life there. For others there is only misery and hardship."

Is one therefore not describing dangers when speaking of the Mysteries? Is it not robbing a man of happiness and of the best part of his life to take him to the portals of the nether-world? Terrible is the responsibility incurred by such an act. And yet ought we to refuse that responsibility? These were the questions which the initiate had to put to himself. He was of opinion that his knowledge bore the same relation to the soul of the people as light does to darkness. But innocent happiness dwells in that darkness, and the Mystics were of opinion that that happiness should not be sacrilegiously interfered with. For what would have happened in the first place if the Mystic had betrayed his secret? He would have uttered words and only words. The feelings and emotions which would have evoked the spirit from the words would have been absent. To do this preparation, exercises, tests, and a complete change in the life of sense were necessary. Without this the hearer would have been hurled into emptiness and nothingness. He would have been deprived of what constituted his happiness, without receiving anything in exchange. One may also say that one could take nothing away from him, for mere words would change nothing in his life of feeling. He would only have been able to feel and experience reality through his senses. Nothing but a terrible misgiving, fatal to life, would be given him. This could only be construed as a crime.

The wisdom of the Mysteries is like a hothouse plant, which must be cultivated and fostered in seclusion. Any one bringing it into the atmosphere of everyday ideas brings it into air in which it cannot flourish. It withers away to nothing before the caustic verdict of modern science and logic. Let us therefore divest ourselves for a time of the education we gained through the microscope and telescope and the habit of thought derived from natural science, and let us cleanse our clumsy hands, which have been too busy with dissecting and experimenting, in order that we may enter the pure temple of the Mysteries. For this a candid and unbiassed attitude of mind is necessary.

The important point for the Mystic is at first the frame of mind in which he approaches that which to him is the highest, the answers to the riddles of existence. Just in our day, when only gross physical science is recognised as containing truth, it is difficult to believe that in the highest things we depend upon the key-note of the soul. Knowledge thereby becomes an intimate personal concern. But this is what it really is to the Mystic. Tell some one the solution of the riddle of the universe! Give it him ready-made! The Mystic will find it to be nothing but empty sound, if the personality does not meet the solution half-way in the right manner. The solution in itself is nothing; it vanishes if the necessary feeling is not kindled at its contact. A divinity approaches you. It is either everything or nothing. Nothing, if you meet it in the frame of mind with which you confront everyday matters. Everything, if you are prepared, and attuned to the meeting. What the Divinity is in itself is a matter which does not affect you; the important point for you is whether it leaves you as it found you or makes another man of you. But this depends entirely on yourself. You must have been prepared by a special education, by a development of the inmost forces of your personality for the work of kindling and releasing what a divinity is able to kindle and release in you. What is brought to you depends on the reception you give to it.

Plutarch has told us about this education, and of the greeting which the Mystic offers the divinity approaching him; "For the god, as it were, greets each one who approaches him, with the words, 'Know thyself,' which is surely no worse than the ordinary greeting, 'Welcome.' Then we answer the divinity in the words, 'Thou art,' and thus we affirm that the true, primordial, and only adequate greeting for him is to declare that he is. In that existence we really have no part here, for every mortal being, situated between birth and destruction, merely manifests an appearance, a feeble and uncertain image of itself. If we try to grasp it with our understanding, it is as when water is tightly compressed and runs over merely through the pressure, spoiling what it touches. For the understanding, pursuing a too definite conception of each being that is subject to accidents and change, loses its way, now in the origin of the being, now in its destruction, and is unable to apprehend anything lasting or really existing. For, as Heraclitus says, we cannot swim twice in the same wave, neither can we lay hold of a mortal being twice in the same state, for, through the violence and rapidity of movement, it is destroyed and recomposed; it comes into being and again decays; it comes and goes. Therefore, that which is becoming can neither attain real existence, because growth neither ceases nor pauses. Change begins in the germ, and forms an embryo; then there appears a child, then a youth, a man, and an old man; the first beginnings and successive ages are continually annulled by the ensuing ones. Hence it is ridiculous to fear one death, when we have already died in so many ways, and are still dying. For, as Heraclitus says, not only is the death of fire the birth of air, and the death of air the birth of water, but the same change may be still more plainly seen in man. The strong man dies when he becomes old, the youth when he becomes a man, the boy on becoming a youth, and the child on becoming a boy. What existed yesterday dies to-day, what is here to-day will die to-morrow. Nothing endures or is a unity, but we become many things, whilst matter wanders around one image, one common form. For if we were always the same, how could we take pleasure in things which formerly did not please us, how could we love and hate, admire and blame opposite things, how could we speak differently and give ourselves up to different passions, unless we were endowed with a different shape, form, and different senses? For no one can rightly come into a different state without change, and one who is changed is no longer the same; but if he is not the same, he no longer exists and is changed from what he was, becoming something else. Sense-perception only led us astray, because we do not know real being, and mistook for it that which is only an appearance."[2]

Plutarch often describes himself as an initiate. What he portrays here is a condition of the life of the Mystic. Man acquires a kind of wisdom by means of which his spirit sees through the illusive character of sense-life. What the senses regard as being, or reality, is plunged into the stream of "becoming"; and man is subject to the same conditions in this respect as all other things in the world. Before the eyes of his spirit he himself dissolves, the sum-total of his being is broken up into parts, into fleeting phenomena. Birth and death lose their distinctive meaning, and become moments of appearing and disappearing, just as much as any other happenings in the world. The Highest cannot be found in the connection between development and decay. It can only be sought in what is really abiding, in what looks back to the past and forward to the future.

To find that which looks (*i.e.* the spirit) backwards and forwards is the first stage of knowledge. This is the spirit, which is manifesting in and through the physical. It has nothing to do with physical growth. It does not come into being and again decay as do sense-phenomena. One who lives entirely in the world of sense carries the spirit latent within him. One who has pierced through the illusion of the world of sense has the spirit within him as a manifest reality. The man who attains to this insight has developed a new principle within him. Something has happened within him as in a plant when it adds a coloured flower to its green leaves. It is true the forces causing the flower to grow were already latent in the plant before the blossom appeared, but they only became effective when this took place. Divine, spiritual forces are latent in the man who lives merely through his senses, but they only become a manifest reality in the initiate. Such is the transformation which takes place in the Mystic. By his development he has added a new element to the world. The world of sense made him a human being endowed with senses, and then left him to himself. Nature had thus fulfilled her mission. What she is able to do with the powers operative in man is exhausted; not so the forces themselves. They lie as though spellbound in the merely natural man and await their release. They cannot release themselves. They fade away to nothing unless man seizes upon them and develops them, unless he calls into actual being what is latent within him.

Nature evolves from the imperfect to the perfect. She leads beings, through a long series of stages, from inanimate matter, through all living forms up to physical man. Man looks around and finds himself a changing being with physical reality, but he also perceives within him the forces from which the physical reality arose. These forces are not what change, for they have given birth to the changing world. They are within man as a sign that there is more life within him than he can physically perceive. What they may make man is not yet there. He feels something flash up within him which created everything, including himself, and he feels that this will inspire him to higher creative activity. This something is within him, it existed before his manifestation in the flesh, and will exist afterwards. By means of it he became, but he may lay hold of it and take part in its creative activity.

Such are the feelings animating the Mystic after initiation. He feels the Eternal and Divine. His activity is to become a part of that divine creative activity. He may say to himself: "I have discovered a higher ego within me, but that ego extends beyond the bounds of my sense-existence. It existed before my birth and will exist after my death. This ego has created from all eternity, it will go on creating in all eternity. My physical personality is a creation of this ego. But it has incorporated me within it, it works within me, I am a part of it. What I henceforth create will be higher than the physical. My personality is only a means for this creative power, for this Divine is within me." Thus did the Mystic experience his birth into the Divine.

The Mystic called the power that flashed up within him a daimon. He was himself the product of this daimon. It seemed to him as though another being had entered him and taken possession of his organs, a being standing between his physical personality and the all-ruling cosmic power, the divinity.

The Mystic sought this—his daimon. He said to himself: "I have become a human being in mighty Nature, but Nature did not complete her task. This completion I must take in hand myself. But I cannot accomplish it in the gross kingdom of nature to which my physical personality belongs. What it is possible to develop in that realm has already been developed. Therefore I must leave this kingdom and take up the building in the realm of the spirit at the point where nature left off. I must create an atmosphere of life not to be found in outer nature."

This atmosphere of life was prepared for the Mystic in the Mystery temples. There the forces slumbering within him were awakened, there he was changed into a higher creative spirit-nature. This transformation was a delicate process. It could not bear the untempered atmosphere of everyday life. But when once it was completed, its result was that the initiate stood as a rock, rising from the eternal and able to defy all storms. But it was impossible for him to reveal his experiences to any one unprepared to receive them.

Plutarch says that the Mysteries gave deep understanding of the true nature of the daimons. And Cicero tells us that from the Mysteries, "When they are explained and traced back to their meaning, we learn the nature of things rather than that of the gods."[3] From such statements we see clearly that there were higher revelations for the Mystics about the nature of things than that which popular religion was able to impart. Indeed we see that the daimons, *i.e.*, spiritual beings, and the gods themselves, needed explaining. Therefore initiates went back to beings of a higher nature than daimons or gods, and this was characteristic of the essence of the wisdom of the Mysteries.

The people represented the gods and daimons in images borrowed from the world of sense-reality. Would not one who had penetrated into the nature of the Eternal doubt about the eternal nature of such gods as these? How could the Zeus of popular imagination be eternal if he bore within him the qualities of a perishable being? One thing was clear to the Mystics, that man arrives at a conception of the gods in a different way from the conception of other things. An object belonging to the outer world compels us to form a very definite idea of it. In contrast to this, we form our conception of the gods in a freer and somewhat arbitrary manner. The control of the outer world is absent. Reflection teaches us that what we conceive as gods is not subject to outer control. This places us in logical uncertainty; we begin to feel that we ourselves are the creators of our gods. Indeed, we ask ourselves how we have arrived at a conception of the universe that goes beyond physical reality. The initiate was obliged to ask himself such questions; his doubts were justified. "Look at all representations of the gods," he might think to himself. "Are they not like the beings we meet in the world of sense? Did not man create them for himself, by giving or withholding from them, in his thought, some quality belonging to beings of the sense-world? The savage lover of the chase creates a heaven in which the gods themselves take part in glorious hunting, and the Greek peopled his Olympus with divine beings whose models were taken from his own surroundings."

The philosopher Xenophanes (B.C. 575-480) drew attention to this fact with a crude logic. We know that the older Greek philosophers were entirely dependent on the wisdom of the Mysteries. We will afterwards prove this in detail, beginning with Heraclitus. What Xenophanes says may at once be taken as the conviction of a Mystic. It runs thus:

"Men who picture the gods as created in their own human forms, give them human senses, voices, and bodies. But if cattle and lions had hands, and knew how to use them, like men, in painting and working, they would paint the forms of the gods and shape their bodies as their own bodies were constituted. Horses would create gods in horse-form, and cattle would make gods like bulls."

Through insight of this kind, man may begin to doubt the existence of anything divine. He may reject all mythology, and only recognise as reality what is forced upon him by his sense-perception. But the Mystic did not become a doubter of this kind. He saw that the doubter would be like a plant were it to say: "My crimson flowers are null and futile, because I am complete within my green leaves. What I may add to them is only adding illusive appearance." Just as little could the Mystic rest content with gods thus created, the gods of the people. If the plant could think, it would understand that the forces which created its green leaves are also destined to create crimson flowers, and it would not rest till it had investigated those forces and come face to face with them. This was the attitude of the Mystic towards the gods of the people. He did not deny them, or say they were illusion; but he knew they had been created by man. The same forces, the same divine element, which are at work in nature, are at work in the Mystic. They create within him images of the gods. He wishes to see the force that creates the gods; it comes from a higher source than these gods. Xenophanes alludes to it thus: "There is one god greater than all gods and men. His form is not like that of mortals, his thoughts are not their thoughts."

This god was also the God of the Mysteries. He might have been called a "hidden God," for man could never find him with his senses only. Look at outer things around you, you will find nothing divine. Exert your reason, you may be able to detect the laws by which things appear and disappear, but even your reason will not show you anything divine. Saturate your imagination with religious feeling, and you may be able to create images which you may take to be gods, but your reason will pull them to pieces, for it will prove to you that you created them yourself, and borrowed the material from the sense-world. So long as you look at outer things in your quality of simply a reasonable being, you must deny the existence of God; for God is hidden from the senses, and from that reason of yours which explains sense-perceptions.

God lies hidden spellbound in the world, and you need His own power to find Him. You must awaken that power in yourself. These are the teachings which were given to the candidate for initiation.

And now there began for him the great cosmic drama with which his life was bound up. The action of the drama meant nothing less than the deliverance of the spellbound god. Where is God? This was the question asked by the soul of the Mystic. God is not existent, but nature exists. And in nature He must be found. There He has found an enchanted grave. It was in a higher sense that the Mystic understood the words "God is love." For God has exalted that love to its climax, He has sacrificed Himself in infinite love, He has poured Himself out, fallen into number in the manifold of nature. Things in nature live and He does not live. He slumbers within them. We are able to awaken Him; if we are to give Him existence, we must deliver Him by the creative power within us.

The candidate now looks unto himself. As latent creative power as yet without existence, the Divine is living in his soul. In the soul is a sacred place where the spellbound god may wake to liberty. The soul is the mother who is able to conceive the god by nature. If the soul allows herself to be impregnated by nature, she will give birth to the divine. God is born from the marriage of the soul with nature,—no longer a "hidden," but a manifest god. He has life, a perceptible life, wandering amongst men. He is the god freed from enchantment, the offspring of the God who was hidden by a spell. He is not the great God, who was and is and is to come, but yet he may be taken, in a certain sense, as the revelation of Him. The Father remains at rest in the unseen; the Son is born to man out of his own soul. Mystical knowledge is thus an actual event in the cosmic process. It is the birth of the Divine. It is an event as real as any natural event, only enacted upon a higher plane.

The great secret of the Mystic is that he himself creates his god, but that he first prepares himself to recognise the god created by him. The uninitiated man has no feeling for the father of that god, for that Father slumbers under a spell. The Son appears to be born of a virgin, the soul having seemingly given birth to him without impregnation. All her other children are conceived by the sense-world. Their father may be seen and touched, having the life of sense. The Divine Son alone is begotten of the hidden, eternal, Divine, Father Himself.

FOOTNOTES:

[2] Plutarch's Moral Works, *On the Inscription EJ at Delphi*, pp. 17-18.

[3] Plutarch, *On the Decline of the Oracles*; Cicero *On the Nature of the Gods*.

III

THE GREEK SAGES BEFORE PLATO IN THE LIGHT OF THE WISDOM OF THE MYSTERIES

Numerous facts combine to show us that the philosophical wisdom of the Greeks rested on the same mental basis as mystical knowledge. We only understand the great philosophers when we approach them with feelings gained through study of the Mysteries. With what veneration does Plato speak of the "secret doctrines" in the *Phædo*. "And it almost seems," says he, "as though those who have appointed the initiations for us are not at all ordinary people, but that for a long time they have been enjoining upon us that any one who reaches Hades without being initiated and sanctified falls into the mire; but that he who is purified and consecrated when he arrives, dwells with the gods. For those who have to do with initiations say that there are many thyrsus-bearers, but few really inspired. These latter are, in my opinion, none other than those who have devoted themselves in the right way to wisdom. I myself have not missed the opportunity of becoming one of these, as far as I was able, but have striven after it in every way."

It is only a man who is putting his own search for wisdom entirely at the disposal of the condition of soul created by initiation who could thus speak of the Mysteries. And there is no doubt that a flood of light is poured on the words of the great Greek philosophers, when we illustrate them from the Mysteries.

The relation of Heraclitus of Ephesus (535-475 B.C.) to the Mysteries is plainly given us in a saying about him, to the effect that his thoughts "were an impassable road," and that any one, entering upon them without being initiated, found only "dimness and darkness," but that, on the other hand, they were "brighter than the sun" for any one introduced to them by a Mystic. And when it is said of his book, that he deposited it in the temple of Artemis, this only means that initiates alone could understand him. (Edmund Pfleiderer has already collected the historical evidence for the relation of Heraclitus to the Mysteries. *Cf.* his book *Die Philosophie des Heraklit von Ephesus im Lichte der Mysterienidee*. Berlin, 1886.) Heraclitus was called "The Obscure," because it was only through the Mysteries that light could be thrown on his intuitive views.

Heraclitus comes before us as a man who took life with the greatest earnestness. We see plainly from his features, if we know how to reconstruct them, that he bore within him intimate knowledge which he knew that words could only indicate, not express. Out of such a temper of mind arose his celebrated utterance, "All things fleet away," which Plutarch explains thus: "We do not dip twice into the same wave, nor can we touch twice the same mortal being. For through abruptness and speed it disperses and brings together, not in succession but simultaneously."

A man who thus thinks has penetrated the nature of transitory things, for he has felt compelled to characterise the essence of transitoriness itself in the clearest terms. Such a description as this could not be given, unless the transitory were being measured by the eternal, and in particular it could not be extended to man without having seen his inner nature. Heraclitus has extended his characterisation to man. "Life and death, waking and sleeping, youth and age are the same; this in changing is that, and that again this." In this sentence there is expressed full knowledge of the illusionary nature of the lower personality. He says still more forcibly, "Life and death are found in our living even as in our dying." What does this mean but that it is only a transient point of view when we value life more than death? Dying is to perish, in order to make way for new life, but the eternal is living in the new life, as in the old. The same eternal appears in transitory life as in death. When we grasp this eternal, we look upon life and death with the same feeling. Life only has a special value when we have not been able to awaken the eternal within us. The saying, "All things fleet away," might be repeated a thousand times, but unless said in this feeling, it is an empty sound. The knowledge of eternal growth is valueless if it does not detach us from temporal growth. It is the turning away from that love of life which impels towards the transitory, which Heraclitus indicates in his utterance, "How can we say about our daily life, 'We are,' when from the standpoint of the eternal we know that 'We are and are not?'" (Cf. *Fragments of Heraclitus*, No. 81.) "Hades and Dionysos are one and the same," says one of the *Fragments*. Dionysos, the god of joy in life, of germination and growth, to whom the Dionysiac festivals are dedicated is, for Heraclitus, the same as Hades, the god of destruction and annihilation. Only one who sees death in life and life in death, and in both the eternal, high above life and death, can view the merits and demerits of existence in the right light. Then even imperfections become justified, for in them too lives the eternal. What they are from the standpoint of the limited lower life, they are only in appearance,—"The gratification of men's wishes is not necessarily a happiness for them. Illness makes health sweet and good, hunger makes food appreciated, and toil rest." "The sea contains the purest and impurest water, drinkable and wholesome for fishes, it is undrinkable and injurious to human beings." Here Heraclitus is not primarily drawing attention to the transitoriness of earthly things, but to the splendour and majesty of the eternal.

Heraclitus speaks vehemently against Homer and Hesiod, and the learned men of his day. He wished to show up their way of thinking, which clings to the transitory only. He did not desire gods endowed with qualities taken from a perishable world, and he could not regard as a supreme science, that science which investigates the growth and decay of things. For him, the eternal speaks out of the perishable, and for this eternal he has a profound symbol. "The harmony of the world returns upon itself, like that of the lyre and the bow." What depths are hidden in this image! By the pressing asunder of forces, and again by the harmonising of these divergent forces, unity is attained. How one sound contradicts another, and yet, together, they produce harmony. If we apply this to the Spiritual world, we have the thought of Heraclitus, "Immortals are mortal, mortals immortal, living the death of mortals, dying the life of the Immortals."

It is man's original fault to direct his cognition to the transitory. Thereby he turns away from the eternal, and life becomes a danger to him. What happens to him, comes to him through life, but its events lose their sting if he ceases to set unconditioned value on life. In that case his innocence is restored to him. It is as though he were from the so-called seriousness of life able to return to his childhood. The adult takes many things seriously with which a child merely plays, but one who really knows, becomes like a child. "Serious" values lose their value, looked at from the standpoint of eternity. Life then seems like a play. On this account does Heraclitus say, "Eternity is a child at play, it is the reign of a child." Where does the original fault lie? In taking with the utmost seriousness what does not deserve to be so taken. God has poured Himself into the universe of things. If we take these things and leave God unheeded, we take them in earnest as "the tombs of God." We should play with them like a child, and should earnestly strive to awaken forth from them God, who sleeps spellbound within them.

Contemplation of the eternal acts like a consuming fire on ordinary illusions about the nature of things. The spirit breaks up thoughts which come through the senses, it fuses them. This is the higher meaning of the Heraclitean thought, that fire is the primary element of all things. This thought is certainly to be taken at first as an ordinary physical explanation of the phenomena of the universe. But no one understands Heraclitus who does not think of him in the same way as Philo, living in the early days of Christianity, thought of the laws of the Bible. "There are people," he says, "who take the written laws *merely* as symbols of spiritual teaching, who diligently search for the latter, but despise the laws themselves. I can only blame such, for they should pay heed to both, to knowledge of the hidden meaning and to observing the obvious one." If the question is discussed whether Heraclitus meant by "fire" physical fire, or whether fire for him was only a symbol of eternal spirit which dissolves and reconstitutes all things, this is putting a wrong construction upon his thought. He meant both and neither of these things. For spirit was also alive, for him, in ordinary fire, and the force which is physically active in fire lives on a higher plane in the human soul, which melts in its crucible mere sense-knowledge, so that out of this the contemplation of the eternal may arise.

It is very easy to misunderstand Heraclitus. He makes Strife the "Father of things," but only of "things," not of the eternal. If there were no contradictions in the world, if the most multifarious interests were not opposing each other, the world of becoming, of transitory things, would not exist. But what is revealed in this antagonism, what is poured forth into it, is not strife but harmony. Just because there is strife in all things, the spirit of the wise should pass over them like a breath of fire, and change them into harmony.

At this point there shines forth one of the great thoughts of Heraclitean wisdom. What is man as a personal being? From the above point of view Heraclitus is able to answer. Man is composed of the conflicting elements into which divinity has poured itself. In this state he finds himself, and beyond this becomes aware of the spirit within him,—the spirit which is rooted in the eternal. But the spirit itself is born, for man, out of the conflict of elements, and it is the first which has to calm them. In man, Nature surpasses her natural limits. It is indeed the same universal force which created antagonism and the mixture of elements which is afterwards, by its wisdom, to do away with the conflict. Here we arrive at the eternal dualism which lives in man, the perpetual antagonism between the temporal and the eternal. Through the eternal he has become something quite definite, and out of this, he is to create something higher. He is both dependent and independent. He can only participate in the eternal Spirit whom he contemplates, in the measure of the compound of elements which that eternal Spirit has effected within him. And it is just on this account that he is called upon to fashion the eternal out of the temporal. The spirit works within him, but works in a special way. It works out of the temporal. It is the peculiarity of the human soul that a temporal thing should be able to work like an eternal one, should grow and increase in power like an eternal thing. This is why the soul is at once like a god and a worm. Man, owing to this, stands in a mid-position between God and animals. The growing and increasing force within him is his daimonic element,—that within him which pushes out beyond himself.

"Man's daimon is his destiny." Thus strikingly does Heraclitus make reference to this fact. He extends man's vital essence far beyond the personal. The personality is the vehicle of the daimon, which is not confined within the limit of the personality, and for which the birth and death of the personality are of no importance. What is the relation of the daimonic element to the personality which comes and goes? The personality is only a form for the manifestation of the daimon.

One who has arrived at this knowledge looks beyond himself, backwards and forwards. The daimonic experiences through which he has passed are enough to prove to him his own immortality. And he can no longer limit his daimon to the one function of occupying his personality, for the latter can only be one of the forms in which the daimon is manifested. The daimon cannot be shut up within one personality, he has power to animate many. He is able to transform himself from one personality into another. The great thought of reincarnation springs as a matter of course from the Heraclitean premises, and not only the thought but the experience of the fact. The thought only paves the way for the experience. One who becomes conscious of the daimonic element within him does not recognise it as innocent and in its first stage. He finds that it has qualities. Whence do they come? Why have I certain natural aptitudes? Because others have already worked upon my daimon. And what becomes of the work which I accomplish in the daimon if I am not to assume that its task ends with my personality? I am working for a future personality. Between me and the Spirit of the Universe, something interposes which reaches beyond me, but is not yet the same as divinity. This something is my daimon. My to-day is only the product of yesterday, my to-morrow will be the product of to-day; in the same way my life is the result of a former and will be the foundation of a future one. Just as mortal man looks back to innumerable yesterdays and forward to many to-morrows, so does the soul of the sage look upon many lives in his past and many in the future. The thoughts and aptitudes I acquired yesterday I am using to-day. Is it not the same with life? Do not people enter upon the horizon of existence with the most diverse capacities? Whence this difference? Does it proceed from nothing?

Our natural sciences take much credit to themselves for having banished miracle from our views of organic life. David Frederick Strauss, in his *Alter und Neuer Glaube*, considers it a great achievement of our day that we no longer think that a perfect organic being is a miracle issuing from nothing. We understand its perfection when we are able to explain it as a development from imperfection. The structure of an ape is no longer a miracle if we assume its ancestors to have been primitive fishes which have been gradually transformed. Let us at least submit to accept as reasonable in the domain of spirit what seems to us to be right in the domain of nature. Is the perfect spirit to have the same antecedents as the imperfect one? Does a Goethe have the same antecedents as any Hottentot? The antecedents of an ape are as unlike those of a fish as are the antecedents of Goethe's mind unlike those of a savage. The spiritual ancestry of Goethe's soul is a different one from that of the savage soul. The soul has grown as well as the body. The daimon in Goethe has more progenitors than the one in a savage. Let us take the doctrine of reincarnation in this sense, and we shall no longer find it unscientific. We shall be able to explain in the right way what we find in our souls, and we shall not take what we find as if created by a miracle. If I can write, it is owing to the fact that I learned to write. No one who has a pen in his hand for the first time can sit down and write offhand. But one who has come into the world with "the stamp of genius," must he owe it to a miracle? No, even the "stamp of genius" must be acquired. It must have been learned. And when it appears in a person, we call it a daimon. This daimon too must have been to school; it acquired in a former life what it puts into force in a later one.

In this form, and this form only, did the thought of eternity pass before the mind of Heraclitus and other Greek sages. There was no question with them of a continuance of the immediate personality after death. Compare some verses of Empedocles (B.C. 490-430). He says of those who accept the data of experience as miracles:

Foolish and ignorant they, and do not reach far with their thinking,
Who suppose that what has not existed can come into being,
Or that something may die away wholly and vanish completely;
Impossible is it that any beginning can come from Not-Being,
Quite impossible also that being can fade into nothing;
For wherever a being is driven, there will it continue to be.
Never will any believe, who has been in these matters instructed,
That spirits of men only live while what is called life here endures,
That only so long do they live, receiving their joys and their sorrows,
But that ere they were born here and when they are dead, they are nothing.

The Greek sage did not even raise the question whether there was an eternal part in man, but only enquired in what this eternal element consisted and how man can nourish and cherish it in himself. For from the outset it was clear to him that man is an intermediate creation between the earthly and the divine. It was not a question of a divine being outside and beyond the world. The divine lives in man but lives in him only in a human way. It is the force urging man to make himself ever more and more divine. Only one who thinks thus can say with Empedocles:

When leaving thy body behind thee, thou soarest into the ether, Then thou becomest a god, immortal, not subject to death.

What may be done for a human life from this point of view? It may be introduced into the magic circle of the eternal. For in man there must be forces which merely natural life does not develop. And the life might pass away unused if the forces remained idle. To open them up, thereby to make man like the divine,—this was the task of the Mysteries. And this was also the mission which the Greek sages set before themselves. In this way we can understand Plato's utterance, that "he who passes unsanctified and uninitiated into the world below will lie in a slough, but that he who arrives there after initiation and purification will dwell with the gods." We have to do here with a conception of immortality, the significance of which lies bound up within the universe. Everything which man undertakes in order to awaken the eternal within him, he does in order to raise the value of the world's existence. The fresh knowledge he gains does not make him an idle spectator of the universe, forming images for himself of what would be there just as much if he did not exist. The force of his knowledge is a higher one, it is one of the creative forces of nature. What flashes up within him spiritually is something divine which was previously under a spell, and which, failing the knowledge he has gained, must have lain fallow and waited for some other exorcist. Thus a human personality does not live in and for itself, but for the world. Life extends far beyond individual existence when looked at in this way. From within such a point of view we can understand utterances like that of Pindar giving a vista of the eternal: "Happy is he who has seen the Mysteries and then descends under the hollow earth. He knows the end of life, and he knows the beginning promised by Zeus."

We understand the proud traits and solitary nature of sages such as Heraclitus. They were able to say proudly of themselves that much had been revealed to them, for they did not attribute their knowledge to their transitory personality, but to the eternal daimon within them. Their pride had as a necessary adjunct the stamp of humility and modesty, expressed in the words, "All knowledge of perishable things is in perpetual flux like the things themselves." Heraclitus calls the eternal universe a play, he could also call it the most serious of realities. But the word "earnest" has lost its force through being applied to earthly experiences. On the other hand, the realisation of "the play of the eternal" leaves man that security in life of which he is deprived by that earnest which has come out of transitory things.

A different conception of the universe from that of Heraclitus grew up, on the basis of the Mysteries, in the community founded by Pythagoras in the 6th century B.C. in Southern Italy. The Pythagoreans saw the basis of things in the numbers and geometrical figures of which they investigated the laws by means of mathematics. Aristotle says of them: "They first studied mathematics, and, quite engrossed in them, they considered the elements of mathematics to be the elements of all things. Now as numbers are naturally the first thing in mathematics, and they thought they saw many resemblances in numbers to things and to development, and certainly more in numbers than in fire, earth, and water, in this way one quality of numbers came to mean for them justice, another, the soul and spirit, another, time, and so on with all the rest. Moreover they found in numbers the qualities and connections of harmony; and thus everything else, in accordance with its whole nature, seemed to be an image of numbers, and numbers seemed to be the first thing in nature."

The mathematical and scientific study of natural phenomena must always lead to a certain Pythagorean habit of thought. When a string of a certain length is struck, a particular sound is produced. If the string is shortened in certain numeric proportions, other sounds will be produced. The pitch of the sounds may be expressed in figures. Physics also expresses colour-relations in figures. When two bodies combine into one substance, it always happens that a certain definite quantity of the one body, expressible in numbers, combines with a certain definite quantity of the other. The Pythagoreans' sense of observation was directed to such arrangements of measures and numbers in nature. Geometrical figures also play a similar rôle. Astronomy, for instance, is mathematics applied to the heavenly bodies. One fact became important to the thought-life of the Pythagoreans. This was that man, quite alone and purely through his mental activity, discovers the laws of numbers and figures, and yet, that when he looks abroad into nature, he finds that things are obeying the same laws which he has ascertained for himself in his own mind. Man forms the idea of an ellipse, and ascertains the laws of ellipses. And the heavenly bodies move according to the laws which he has established. (It is not, of course, a question here of the astronomical views of the Pythagoreans. What may be said about these may equally be said of Copernican views in the connection now being dealt with.) Hence it follows as a direct consequence that the achievements of the human soul are not an activity apart from the rest of the world, but that in those achievements the cosmic laws are expressed. The Pythagoreans said: "The senses show man physical phenomena, but they do not show the harmonious order which these things follow." The human mind must first find that harmonious order within itself, if it wishes to behold it in the outer world. The deeper meaning of the world, that which bears sway within it as an eternal, law-obeying necessity, this makes its appearance in the human soul and becomes a present reality there. THE MEANING OF THE UNIVERSE IS REVEALED in the soul. This meaning is not to be found in what we see, hear, and touch, but in what the soul brings up to the light from its own unseen depths. The eternal laws are thus hidden in the depths of the soul. If we descend there, we shall find the Eternal. God, the eternal harmony of the world, is in the human soul. The soul-element is not limited to the bodily substance which is enclosed within the skin, for what is born in the soul is nothing less than the laws by which worlds revolve in celestial space. The soul is not in the personality. The personality only serves as the organ through which the order which pervades cosmic space may express itself. There is something of the spirit of Pythagoras in what one of the Fathers, Gregory of Nyssa, said: "It is said that human nature is something small and limited, and that God is infinite, and it is asked how the finite can embrace the infinite. But who dares to say that the infinity of the Godhead is limited by the boundary of the flesh, as though by a vessel? For not even during our lifetime is the spiritual nature confined within the boundaries of the flesh. The mass of the body, it is true, is limited by neighbouring parts, but the soul reaches out freely into the whole of creation by the movements of thought."

The soul is not the personality, the soul belongs to infinity. From such a point of view the Pythagoreans must have considered that only fools could imagine the soul-force to be exhausted with the personality.

For them, too, as for Heraclitus, the essential point was the awakening of the eternal in the personal. Knowledge for them meant intercourse with the eternal. The more man brought the eternal element within him into existence, the greater must he necessarily seem to the Pythagoreans. Life in their community consisted in holding intercourse with the eternal. The object of the Pythagorean education was to lead the members of the community to that intercourse. The education was therefore a philosophical initiation, and the Pythagoreans might well say that by their manner of life they were aiming at a goal similar to that of the cults of the Mysteries.

IV

PLATO AS A MYSTIC

The importance of the Mysteries to the spiritual life of the Greeks may be realised from Plato's conception of the universe. There is only one way of understanding him thoroughly. It is to place him in the light which streams forth from the Mysteries.

Plato's later disciples, the Neo-Platonists, credit him with a secret doctrine which he imparted only to those who were worthy, and which he conveyed under the "seal of secrecy." His teaching was looked upon as mysterious in the same sense as the wisdom of the Mysteries. Even if the seventh Platonic letter is not from his hand, as is alleged, it does not signify for our present purpose, for it does not matter whether it was he or another who gave utterance to the view expressed in this letter. This view is of the essence of Plato's philosophy. In the letter we read as follows: "This much I may say about all those who have written or may hereafter write as if they knew the aim of my work,—that no credence is to be attached to their words, whether they obtained their information from me, or from others, or invented it themselves. I have written nothing on this subject, nor would anything be allowed to appear. This kind of thing cannot be expressed in words like other teaching, but needs a long study of the subject and a making oneself one with it. Then it is as though a spark leaped up and kindled a light in the soul which thereafter is able to keep itself alight." This utterance might only indicate the writer's powerlessness to express his meaning in words,—a mere personal weakness,—if the idea of the Mysteries were not to be found in them. The subject on which Plato had not written and would never write, must be something about which all writing would be futile. It must be a feeling, a sentiment, an experience, which is not gained by instantaneous communication, but by making oneself one with it, in heart and soul. The reference is to the inner education which Plato was able to give those he selected. For them, fire flashed forth from his words, for others, only thoughts.

The manner of our approach to Plato's *Dialogues* is not a matter of indifference. They will mean more or less to us, according to our spiritual condition. Much more passed from Plato to his disciples than the literal meaning of his words. The place where he taught his listeners thrilled in the atmosphere of the Mysteries. His words awoke overtones in higher regions, which vibrated with them, but these overtones needed the atmosphere of the Mysteries, or they died away without having been heard.

In the centre of the world of the Platonic Dialogues stands the personality of Socrates. We need not here touch upon the historical aspect of that personality. It is a question of the character of Socrates as it appears in Plato. Socrates is a person consecrated by his dying for truth. He died as only an initiate can die, as one to whom death is merely a moment of life like other moments. He approaches death as he would any other event in existence. His attitude towards it was such that even in his friends the feelings usual on such an occasion were not aroused. Phædo says this in the *Dialogue on the Immortality of the Soul*: "Truly I found myself in the strangest state of mind. I had no compassion for him, as is usual at the death of a dear friend. So happy did the man appear to me in his demeanour and speech, so steadfast and noble was his end, that I was confident that he was not going to Hades without a divine mission, and that even there it would be as well with him as it is with any one anywhere. No tender-hearted emotion overcame me, as might have been expected at such a mournful event, nor on the other hand was I in a cheerful mood, as is usual during philosophical pursuits, and although our conversation was of this nature; but I found myself in a wondrous state of mind and in an unwonted blending of joy and grief when I reflected that this man was about to die." The dying Socrates instructs his disciples about immortality. His personality, which had learned by experience the worthlessness of life, furnishes a kind of proof quite different from logic and arguments founded on reason. It seems as if it were not a man speaking, for this man was passing away, but as if it were the voice of eternal truth itself, which had taken up its abode in a perishable personality. Where a mortal being is dissolving into nothing, there seems to be a breath of the air in which it is possible for eternal harmonies to resound.

We hear no logical proofs of immortality. The whole discourse is designed to lead the friends where they may behold the eternal. Then they will need no proofs. Would it be necessary to prove that a rose is red, to one who has one before him? Why should it be necessary to prove that spirit is eternal, to one whose eyes we have opened to behold spirit? Experiences, inner events, Socrates points to them, and first of all to the experience of wisdom itself.

What does he desire who aspires after wisdom? He wishes to free himself from what the senses offer him in every-day perception. He seeks for the spirit in the sense-world. Is not this a fact which may be compared with dying? "For," according to Socrates, "those who occupy themselves with philosophy in the right way are really striving after nothing else than to die and to be dead, without this being perceived by others. If this is true, it would be strange if, after having aimed at this all through life, when death itself comes they should be indignant at that which they have so long striven after and taken pains about." To corroborate this, Socrates asks one of his friends: "Does it seem to you befitting a philosopher to take trouble about so-called fleshly pleasures, such as eating and drinking? or about sexual pleasures? And do you think that such a man pays much heed to other bodily needs? To have fine clothes, shoes, and other bodily adornments,—do you think he considers or scorns this more than utmost necessity demands? Does it not seem to you that it should be such a man's whole preoccupation not to turn his thoughts to the body, but as much as possible away from it and towards the soul? Therefore this is the first mark of the philosopher, that he, more than all other men, relieves his soul of association with the body."

On this subject Socrates has something more to say, *i.e.*, that aspiration after wisdom has this much in common with dying, that it turns man away from the physical. But whither does he turn? Towards the spiritual. But can he desire the same from spirit as from the senses? Socrates thus expresses himself on this point: "But how is it with reasonable knowledge itself? Is the body a hindrance or not, if we take it as a companion in our search for knowledge? I mean, do sight and hearing procure man any truth? Or is what the poets sing meaningless, that we see and hear nothing clearly?... When does the soul catch sight of truth? For when it tries to examine something with the help of the body, it is manifestly deceived by the latter."

Everything of which we are cognisant by means of our bodily senses appears and disappears. And it is this appearing and disappearing which is the cause of our being deceived. But when with our reasonable intelligence we look deeper into things, the eternal element in them is revealed to us. Thus the senses do not offer us the eternal in its true form. The moment we trust them implicitly they deceive us. They cease to deceive us if we confront them with our thinking insight and submit what they tell us to its examination.

But how could our thinking insight sit in judgment on the declarations of the senses, unless there were something living within it which transcends sense-perception? Therefore the truth or falsity in things is decided by something within us which opposes the physical body and is consequently not subject to its laws. First of all, it cannot be subject to the laws of growth and decay. For this something contains truth within it. Now truth cannot have a yesterday and a to-day, it cannot be one thing one day and another the next, like objects of sense. Therefore truth must be something eternal. And when the philosopher turns away from the perishable things of sense and towards truth, he is turning towards an eternal element that lives within him. If we immerse ourselves wholly in spirit, we shall live wholly in truth. The things of sense around us are no longer present merely in their physical form. "And he accomplishes this most perfectly," says Socrates, "who approaches everything as much as possible with the spirit only, without either looking round when he is thinking, or letting any other sense interrupt his reflecting; but who, making use of pure thought only, strives to grasp everything as it is in itself, separating it as much as possible from eyes and ears, in short from the whole body, which only disturbs the soul and does not allow it to attain truth and insight when associated with the soul.... Now is not death the release and separation of the soul from the body? And it is only true philosophers who are always striving to release the soul as far as they can. This, therefore, is the philosopher's vocation, to deliver and separate the soul from the body.... Therefore it would be foolish if a man, who all his life has taken measures to be as near death as possible, should, when it comes, rebel against it.... In truth the real seekers after wisdom aspire to die, and of all men they are those who least fear death." Moreover Socrates bases all higher morality on liberation from the body. He who only follows what his body ordains is not moral. Who is valiant? asks Socrates. He is valiant who does not obey his body but the demands of his spirit when these demands imperil the body. And who is temperate? Is not this he who "does not let himself be carried away by desires, but who maintains an indifferent and moral demeanour with regard to them. Therefore are not those alone temperate who set least value on the body and live in the love of wisdom?" And so it is, in the opinion of Socrates, with all virtues.

Thence Socrates goes on to characterise intellectual cognition. What is it after all, to cognise? Undoubtedly we arrive at it by forming judgments. I form a judgment about some object; for instance, I say to myself, what is in front of me is a tree. How do I arrive at saying that? I can only do it if I already know what a tree is. I must remember my conception of a tree. A tree is a physical object. If I remember a tree, I therefore remember a physical object. I say of something that it is a tree, if it resembles other things which I have previously observed and which I know to be trees. Memory is the medium for this knowledge. It makes it possible for me to compare the various objects of sense. But this does not exhaust my knowledge. If I see two similar things, I form a judgment and say, these things are alike. Now, in reality, two things are never exactly alike. I can only find a likeness in certain respects. The idea of a perfect similarity therefore arises within me without having its correspondence in reality. And this idea helps me to form a judgment, as memory helps me to a judgment and to knowledge. Just as one tree reminds me of others, so am I reminded of the idea of similarity by looking at two things from a certain point of view. Thoughts and memories therefore arise within me which are not due to physical reality.

All kinds of knowledge not borrowed from sense-reality are grounded on such thoughts. The whole of mathematics consists of them. He would be a bad geometrician who could only bring into mathematical relations what he can see with his eyes and touch with his hands. Thus we have thoughts which do not originate in perishable nature, but arise out of the spirit. And it is these that bear in them the mark of eternal truth. What mathematics teach will be eternally true, even if to-morrow the whole cosmic system should fall into ruins and an entirely new one arise. Conditions might prevail in another cosmic system, to which our present mathematical truths would not be applicable, but these would be none the less true in themselves.

It is only when the soul is alone with itself that it can bring forth these eternal truths. It is at these times related to the true and eternal, and not to the ephemeral and apparent. Hence Socrates says: "When the soul returning into itself reflects, it goes straight to what is pure and everlasting and immortal and like unto itself; and being related to this, cleaves unto it when the soul is alone, and is not hindered. And then the soul rests from its mistakes, and is like unto itself, even as the eternal is, with whom the soul is now in touch. This state of soul is called wisdom.... Look now whether it does not follow from all that has been said, that the soul is most like the divine, immortal, reasonable, unique, indissoluble, what is always the same and like unto itself; and that on the other hand the body most resembles what is human and mortal, unreasonable, multiform, soluble, never the same nor remaining equal to itself.... If, therefore, this be so, the soul goes to what is like itself, to the immaterial, to the divine, immortal, reasonable. There it attains to bliss, freed from error and ignorance, from fear and undisciplined love and all other human evils. There it lives, as the initiates say, for the remaining time truly with God."

It is not within the scope of this book to indicate all the ways in which Socrates leads his friends to the eternal. They all breathe the same spirit. They all tend to show that man finds one thing when he goes the way of transitory sense-perception, and another when his spirit is alone with itself. It is to this original nature of spirit that Socrates points his hearers. If they find it, they see with their own spiritual eyes that it is eternal. The dying Socrates does not prove the immortality of the soul, he simply lays bare the nature of the soul. And then it comes to light that growth and decay, birth and death, have nothing to do with the soul. The essence of the soul lies in the true, and this can neither come into being nor perish. The soul has no more to do with the becoming than the straight has with the crooked. But death belongs to the becoming. Therefore the soul has nothing to do with death. Must we not say of what is immortal, that it admits of mortality as little as does the straight of the crooked? Starting from this point, "must we not ask," adds Socrates, "that if the immortal is imperishable, is it not impossible for the soul to come to an end when death arrives? For from what has been already shown, it does not admit of death, nor can it die any more than three can be an even number."

Let us review the whole development of this dialogue, in which Socrates brings his hearers to behold the eternal in human personality. The hearers accept his thoughts, and they look into themselves to see if they can find in their inner experiences something which assents to his ideas. They make the objections which strike them. What has happened to the hearers when the dialogue is finished? They have found something within them which they did not possess before. They have not merely accepted an abstract truth, but they have gone through a development. Something has come to life in them which was not living in them before. Is not this to be compared with an initiation? And does not this throw light on the reason for Plato's setting forth his philosophy in the form of conversation? These dialogues are nothing else than the literary form of the events which took place in the sanctuaries of the Mysteries. We are convinced of this from what Plato himself says in many passages. Plato wished to be, as a philosophical teacher, what the initiator into the Mysteries was, as far as this was compatible with the philosophical manner of communication. It is evident how Plato feels himself in harmony with the Mysteries! He only thinks he is on the right path when it is taking him where the Mystic is to be led. He thus expresses himself on the subject in the Timæus. "All those who are of right mind invoke the gods for their small or great enterprises; but we who are engaged in teaching about the universe,—how far it is created and uncreated,—have the special duty, if we have not quite lost our way, to call upon and implore the gods and goddesses that we may teach everything first in conformity with their spirit, and next in harmony with ourselves." And Plato promises those who follow this path, that divinity, as a deliverer, will grant them illuminating teaching as the conclusion of their devious and wandering researches.

It is especially the *Timæus* that reveals to us how the Platonic cosmogony is connected with the Mysteries. At the very beginning of this dialogue there is mention of an initiation. Solon is initiated by an Egyptian priest into the formation of the worlds, and the way in which eternal truths are symbolically expressed in traditional myths. "There have already been many and various destructions of part of the human race," says the Egyptian priest to Solon, "and there will be more in the future; the most extensive by fire and water, other lesser ones through countless other causes. It is also related in your country that Phaëthon, the son of Helios, once mounted his father's chariot, and as he did not know how to drive it, everything on the earth was burnt up, and he himself slain by lightning. This sounds like a fable, but it contains the truth of the change in the movements of the celestial bodies revolving round the earth and of the annihilation of everything on the earth by much fire. This annihilation happens periodically, after the lapse of certain long periods of time." This passage in the *Timæus* contains a plain indication of the attitude of the initiate towards folk-myths. He recognises the truths hidden in their images.

The drama of the formation of the world is brought before us in the *Timæus*. Any one who will follow up the traces which lead to this formation of the cosmos arrives at a dim apprehension of the primordial force from which all things proceeded. "Now it is difficult to find the Creator and Father of the universe, and when we have found Him, it is impossible to speak about Him so that all may understand." The Mystic knew what this "impossibility" means. It points to the divine drama. God is not present in what belongs merely to the senses and understanding. In those He is only present as nature. He is under a spell in nature. Only one who awakens the divine within himself is able to approach Him. Thus He cannot at once be made comprehensible to all. But even to one who approaches Him, He does not appear Himself. The *Timæus* says that also. The Father made the universe out of the body and soul of the world. He mixed together, in harmony and perfect proportions, the elements which came into being when He, pouring Himself out, gave up His separate existence. Thereby the body of the world came into being, and stretched upon it, in the form of a cross, is the soul of the world. It is what is divine in the world. It found the death of the cross so that the world might come into existence. Plato may therefore call nature the tomb of the divine, a grave, however, in which nothing dead lies but the eternal, to which death only gives the opportunity of bringing into expression the omnipotence of life. And man sees nature in the right light when he approaches it in order to release the crucified soul of the world. It must rise again from its death, from its spell. Where can it come to life again? Only in the soul of initiated man. Then wisdom finds its right relation to the cosmos. The resurrection, the liberation of God, that is wisdom. In the *Timæus* the development of the world is traced from the imperfect to the perfect. An ascending process is represented imaginatively. Beings are developed. God reveals Himself in their development. Evolution is the resurrection of God from the tomb. Within evolution, man appears. Plato shows that in man there is something special. It is true the whole world is divine, and man is not more divine than other beings. But in other beings God is present in a hidden way, in man he is manifest. At the end of the *Timæus* we read: "And now we might assert that our study of the universe has attained its end, for after the world was provided and filled with mortal and immortal living beings, it, this one and only begotten world, has itself become a visible being embracing everything visible, and an image of the Creator. It has become the God perceptible to the senses, and the greatest and best world, the fairest and most perfect which there could be." But this one and only begotten world would not be perfect if the image of its Creator were not to be found amongst the images it contains. This image can only be engendered in the human soul. Not the Father Himself, but the Son, God's offspring, living in the soul, and being like unto the Father, him man can bring forth.

Philo, of whom it was said that he was the resurrected Plato, characterised as the "Son of God" the wisdom born out of man, which lives in the soul and contains the reason existing in the world. This cosmic reason, or Logos, appears as the book in which "everything in the world is recorded and delineated." It also appears as the Son of God, "following in the paths of the Father, and creating forms, looking at their archetypes." The platonising Philo addresses this Logos as Christ, "As God is the first and only king of the universe, the way to Him is rightly called the 'Royal Road.' Consider this road to be philosophy ... the road which the company of the ancient ascetics took, who turned away from the entangling fascination of pleasure and devoted themselves to the noble and earnest cultivation of the beautiful. The law names this Royal Road, which we call true philosophy, God's word and spirit."

It is like an initiation to Philo when he enters upon this path, in order to meet the Logos who, to him, is the Son of God. "I do not shrink from relating what has happened to me innumerable times. Often when I wished to put my philosophical thoughts in writing, in my accustomed way, and saw quite clearly what was to be set down, I nevertheless found my mind barren and rigid, so that I was obliged to desist without having accomplished anything, and seemed to be hampered with idle fancies. At the same time I could not but marvel at the power of the reality of thought, with which it rests to open and to close the womb of the human soul. Another time, however, I would begin empty and arrive, without any trouble, at fulness. Thoughts came flying like snowflakes or grains of corn invisibly from above, and it was as though divine power took hold of me and inspired me, so that I did not know where I was, who was with me, who I was, or what I was saying or writing; for just then the flow of ideas was given me, a delightful clearness, keen insight, and lucid mastery of material, as if the inner eye were able to see everything with the greatest distinctness."

This is a description of a path to knowledge so expressed that we see that any one taking this path is conscious of flowing in one current with the divine, when the Logos becomes alive within him. This is also expressed clearly in the words: "When the spirit, moved by love, takes its flight into the most holy, soaring joyously on divine wings, it forgets everything else and itself. It only clings to and is filled with that of which it is the satellite and servant, and to this it offers the incense of the most sacred and chaste virtue."

There are only two ways for Philo. Either man follows the world of sense, that is, what observation and intellect offer, in which case he limits himself to his personality and withdraws from the cosmos; or he becomes conscious of the universal cosmic force, and experiences the eternal within his personality. "He who wishes to escape from God falls into his own hands. For there are two things to be considered, the universal Spirit which is God, and one's own spirit. The latter flees to and takes refuge in the universal Spirit, for one who goes beyond his own spirit says that it is nothing and connects everything with God; but one who avoids God, abolishes the First Cause, and makes himself the cause of everything which happens."

The Platonic view of the universe sets out to be knowledge which by its very nature is also religion. It brings knowledge into relation with the highest to which man can attain through his feelings. Plato will only allow knowledge to hold good when feeling may be completely satisfied in it. It is then more than science, it is the substance of life. It is a higher man within man, that man of which the personality is only an image. Within man is born a being who surpasses him, a primordial, archetypal man, and this is another secret of the Mysteries brought to expression in the Platonic philosophy. Hippolytus, one of the Early Fathers, alludes to this secret. "This is the great secret of the Samothracians (who were guardians of a certain Mystery-cult), which cannot be expressed and which only the initiates know. But these latter speak in detail of Adam, as the primordial, archetypal man."

The Platonic *Dialogue on Love*, or the *Symposium*, also represents an initiation. Here love appears as the herald of wisdom. If wisdom, the eternal word, the Logos, is the Son of the Eternal Creator of the cosmos, love is related to the Logos as a mother. Before even a spark of the light of wisdom can flash up in the human soul, a dim impulse or desire for the divine must be present in it. Unconsciously the divine must draw man to what afterwards, when raised into his consciousness, constitutes his supreme happiness. What Heraclitus calls the "daimon" in man (see p. 49) is connected with the idea of love. In the *Symposium*, people of the most various ranks and views of life speak about love,—the ordinary man, the politician, the scientific man, the satiric poet Aristophanes, and the tragic poet Agathon. They each have their own view of love, in keeping with their different experiences of life. The way in which they express themselves shows the stage at which their "daimon" has arrived (*cf.* p. 49). By love one being is attracted to another. The multiplicity, the diversity of the things into which divine unity was poured, aspires towards unity and harmony through love. Thus love has something divine in it, and owing to this, each individual can only understand it as far as he participates in the divine.

After these men and others at different degrees of maturity have given utterance to their ideas about love, Socrates takes up the word. He considers love from the point of view of a man in search of knowledge. For him, it is not a divinity, but it is something which leads man to God. Eros, or love, is for him not divine, for a god is perfect, and therefore possesses the beautiful and good; but Eros is only the desire for the beautiful and good. He thus stands between man and God. He is a "daimon," a mediator between the earthly and the divine.

It is significant that Socrates does not claim to be giving his own thoughts when speaking of love. He says he is only relating what a woman once imparted to him as a revelation. It was through mantic art that he came to his conception of love. Diotima, the priestess, awakened in Socrates the daimonic force which was to lead him to the divine. She initiated him.

This passage in the *Symposium* is highly suggestive. Who is the "wise woman" who awakened the daimon in Socrates? She is more than a merely poetic mode of expression. For no wise woman on the physical plane could awaken the daimon in the soul, unless the daimonic force were latent in the soul itself. It is surely in Socrates' own soul that we must also look for this "wise woman." But there must be a reason why that which brings the daimon to life within the soul should appear as an outward being on the physical plane. The force cannot work in the same way as the forces which may be observed in the soul, as belonging to and native to it. We see that it is the soul-force which precedes the coming of wisdom which Socrates represents as a "wise woman." It is the mother-principle which gives birth to the Son of God, Wisdom, the Logos. The unconscious soul-force which brings the divine into the consciousness is here represented as the feminine element. The soul which as yet is without wisdom is the mother of what leads to the divine. This brings us to an important conception of mysticism. The soul is recognised as the mother of the divine. Unconsciously it leads man to the divine, with the inevitableness of a natural force.

This conception throws light on the view of Greek mythology taken in the Mysteries. The world of the gods is born in the soul. Man looks upon what he creates in images as his gods (*cf.* p. 33). But he must force his way through to another conception. He must transmute into divine images the divine force which is active within him before the creation of those images. Behind the divine appears the mother of the divine, which is nothing else than the original force of the human soul. Thus side by side with the gods, man represents goddesses.

Let us look at the myth of Dionysos in this light. Dionysos is the son of Zeus and a mortal mother, Semele. Zeus wrests the still immature child from its mother when she is slain by lightning, and shelters it in his own side till it is ready to be born. Hera, the mother of the gods, incites the Titans against Dionysos, and they tear him in pieces. But Pallas Athene rescues his heart, which is still beating, and brings it to Zeus. Out of it he engenders his son for the second time.

In this myth we can accurately trace a process which is enacted in the depths of the human soul. Interpreting it in the manner of the Egyptian priest who instructed Solon about the nature of myths (*cf.* p. 78 *et seq.*), we might say, it is related that Dionysos was the son of a god and of a mortal mother, that he was torn in pieces and afterwards born again. This sounds like a fable, but it contains the truth of the birth of the divine and its destiny in the human soul. The divine unites itself with the earthly, temporal human soul. As soon as the divine, Dionysiac element stirs within the soul, it feels a violent desire for its own true spiritual form. Ordinary consciousness, which once again appears in the form of a female goddess, Hera, becomes jealous at the birth of the divine out of the higher consciousness. It arouses the lower nature of man (the Titans). The still immature divine child is torn in pieces. Thus the divine child is present in man as intellectual science broken up. But if there be enough of the higher wisdom (Zeus) in man to be active, it nurses and cherishes the immature child, which is then born again as a second son of God (Dionysos). Thus from science, which is the fragmentary divine force in man, is born undivided wisdom, which is the Logos, the son of God and of a mortal mother, of the perishable human soul, which unconsciously aspires after the divine. As long as we see in all this merely a process in the soul and look upon it as a picture of this process, we are a long way from the spiritual reality which is enacted in it. In this spiritual reality the soul is not merely experiencing something in itself, but it has been released from itself and is taking part in a cosmic event, which is not enacted within the soul, in reality, but outside it.

Platonic wisdom and Greek myths are closely linked together, so too are the myths and the wisdom of the Mysteries. The created gods were the object of popular religion, the history of their origin was the secret of the Mysteries. No wonder that it was held to be dangerous to "betray" the Mysteries, for thereby the origin of the gods of the people was "betrayed." And a right understanding of that origin is salutary, a misunderstanding is injurious.

V

THE WISDOM OF THE MYSTERIES AND THE MYTH

The Mystic sought forces and beings within himself which are unknown to man as long as he remains in the ordinary attitude towards life. The Mystic puts the great question about his own spiritual forces and the laws which transcend the lower nature. A man of ordinary views of life, bounded by the senses and logic, creates gods for himself, or when he gets to the point of seeing that he has made them, he disclaims them. The Mystic knows that he creates gods, he knows why he creates them, he sees, so to say, behind the natural law which makes man create them. It is as though a plant suddenly became conscious, and learned the laws of its growth and development. As it is, it develops in lovely unconsciousness. If it knew about the laws of its own being, its relation to itself would be completely changed. What the lyric poet feels when he sings about a plant, what the botanist thinks when he investigates its laws, this would hover before a conscious plant as an ideal of itself.

It is thus with the Mystic with regard to the laws, the forces working within him. As one who knew, he was forced to create something divine beyond himself. And the initiates took up the same attitude to that which the people had created beyond nature; that is to the world of popular gods and myths. They wanted to penetrate the laws of this world of gods and myths. Where the people saw the form of a god, or a myth, they looked for a higher truth.

Let us take an example. The Athenians had been forced by the Cretan king Minos to deliver up to him every eight years seven boys and seven girls. These were thrown as food to a terrible monster, the Minotaur. When the mournful tribute was to be paid for the third time, the king's son Theseus accompanied it to Crete. On his arrival there, Ariadne, the daughter of Minos interested herself in him. The Minotaur dwelt in the labyrinth, a maze from which no one could extricate himself who had once got in. Theseus desired to deliver his native city from the shameful tribute. For this purpose he had to enter the labyrinth into which the monster's booty was usually thrown, and to kill the Minotaur. He undertook the task, overcame the formidable foe, and succeeded in regaining the open air with the aid of a ball of thread which Ariadne had given him.

The Mystic had to discover how the creative human mind comes to weave such a story. As the botanist watches the growth of plants in order to discover its laws, so did the Mystic watch the creative spirit. He sought for a truth, a nucleus of wisdom where the people had invented a myth.

Sallust discloses to us the attitude of a mystical sage towards a myth of this kind. "We might call the whole world a myth," says he, "which contains bodies and things visibly, and souls and spirits in a hidden manner. If the truth about the gods were taught to all, the unintelligent would disdain it from not understanding it, and the more capable would make light of it. But if the truth is given in a mystical veil, it is assured against contempt and serves as a stimulus to philosophic thinking."

When the truth contained in a myth was sought by an initiate, he was conscious of adding something which did not exist in the consciousness of the people. He was aware of being above that consciousness, as a botanist is above a growing plant. Something was expressed which was different from what was present in the mythical consciousness, but it was looked upon as a deeper truth, symbolically expressed in the myth. Man is confronted with his own sense-nature in the form of a hostile monster. He sacrifices to it the fruits of his personality, and the monster devours them, and continues to do so till the conqueror (Theseus) awakes in man. His intuition spins the thread by means of which he finds his way again when he repairs to the maze of the senses in order to slay his enemy. The mystery of human knowledge itself is expressed in this conquering of the senses. The initiate knows that mystery. It points to a force in human personality unknown to ordinary consciousness, but nevertheless active within it. It is the force which creates the myth, which has the same structure as mystical truth. This truth finds its symbol in the myth.

What then is to be found in the myths? In them is a creation of the spirit, of the unconsciously creative soul. The soul has well-defined laws. In order to create beyond itself, it must work in a certain direction. At the mythological stage it does this in images, but these are built up according to the laws of the soul. We might also say that when the soul advances beyond the stage of mythological consciousness to deeper truths, these bear the same stamp as did the myths, for one and the same force was at work in their formation.

Plotinus, the philosopher of the Neo-Platonic school (A.D. 204-269), speaks of this relation of mythical representation to higher knowledge in reference to the priest-sages of Egypt. "Whether as the result of rigorous investigations, or whether instinctively when imparting their wisdom, the Egyptian sages do not use, for expressing their teaching and precepts, written signs which are imitations of voice and speech; but they draw pictures, and in the outlines of these they record, in their temples, the thought contained in each thing, so that every picture contains knowledge and wisdom, and is a definite truth and a complete whole, although there is no explanation nor discussion. Afterwards the contents of the picture are drawn out of it and expressed in words, and the cause is found why it is as it is, and not otherwise."

If we wish to find out the connection of mysticism with mythical narratives, we must see what relationship to them there is in the views of the great thinkers, those who knew their wisdom to be in harmony with the methods of the Mysteries. We find such harmony in Plato in the fullest degree. His explanations of myths and his application of them in his teaching may be taken as a model (*cf.* p. 78 *et seq.*). In the *Phædrus*, a dialogue on the soul, the myth of Boreas is introduced. This divine being, who was seen in the rushing wind, one day saw the fair Orithyia, daughter of the Attic king Erectheus, gathering flowers with her companions. Seized with love for her, he carried her off to his grotto. Plato, by the mouth of Socrates, rejects a rationalist interpretation of this myth. According to this explanation, an outward, natural fact is poetically symbolised by the narrative. A hurricane seized the king's daughter and hurled her over the rocks. "Interpretations of this sort," says Socrates, "are learned sophistries, however popular and usual they may be.... For one who has pulled to pieces one of these mythological forms must, to be consistent, elucidate sceptically and explain naturally all the rest in the same way.... But even if such a labour could be accomplished, it would in any case be no proof of superior talents in the one carrying it out, but only of superficial wit, boorish wisdom, and ridiculous haste.... Therefore I leave on one side all such enquiries, and believe what is generally thought about the myths. I do not examine them, as I have just said, but I examine myself to see whether I too may perhaps be a monster, more complicated and therefore more disordered than the chimæra, more savage than Typhon, or whether I represent a more docile and simple being, to whom some particle of a virtuous and divine nature has been given."

We see from this that Plato does not approve of a rationalistic and merely intellectual interpretation of myths. This attitude must be compared with the way in which he himself uses myths in order to express himself through them. When he speaks of the life of the soul, when he leaves the paths of the transitory and seeks the eternal in the soul, when, therefore, images borrowed from sense-perception and reasoning thought can no longer be used, then Plato has recourse to the myth. *Phædrus* treats of the eternal in the soul, which is portrayed as a car drawn by two horses winged all over, and driven by a charioteer. One horse is patient and docile, the other wild and headstrong. If an obstacle comes in the way of the car the troublesome horse takes the opportunity of impeding the docile one and defying the driver. When the car arrives where it has to follow the gods up the celestial steep, the intractable horse throws the team into confusion. If it is less strong than the good horse, it is overcome, and the car is able to go on into the supersensible realm. It thus happens that the soul can never ascend without difficulties into the kingdom of the divine. Some souls rise more to the vision of eternity, some less. The soul which has seen the world beyond remains safe until the next journey. One who, on account of the intractable horse, has not seen beyond, must try again on the next journey. These journeys signify the various incarnations of the soul. One journey signifies the life of the soul in one personality. The wild horse represents the lower nature, the docile one the higher nature; the driver, the soul longing for union with the divine.

Plato resorts to the myth in order to describe the course of the eternal spirit through its various transformations. In the same way he has recourse, in other writings, to symbolical narrative, in order to portray the inner nature of man, which is not perceptible to the senses.

Plato is here in complete harmony with the mythical and allegorical manner of expression used by others. For instance there is in ancient Hindu literature a parable attributed to Buddha.

A man very much attached to life, who seeks sensuous pleasures and will die at no price is pursued by four serpents. He hears a voice commanding him to feed and bathe the serpents from time to time. The man runs away, fearing the serpents. Again he hears a voice, warning him that he is pursued by five murderers. Once more he escapes. A voice calls his attention to a sixth murderer, who is about to behead him with a sword. Again he flees. He comes to a deserted village. There he hears a voice telling him that robbers are shortly going to plunder the village. Having again escaped, he comes to a great flood. He feels unsafe where he is, and out of straw, wood, and leaves he makes a basket in which he arrives at the other shore. Now he is safe, he is a Brahmin.

The meaning of this allegory is that man has to pass through the most various states before attaining to the divine. The four serpents represent the four elements, fire, water, earth, and air. The five murderers are the five senses. The deserted village is the soul which has escaped from sense-impressions, but is not yet safe if it is alone with itself, for if its lower nature lays hold of it, it must perish. Man must construct for himself the boat which is to carry him over the flood of the transitory from the one shore, the sense-nature, to the other, the eternal, divine world.

Let us look at the Egyptian mystery of Osiris in this light. Osiris had gradually become one of the most important Egyptian divinities; he supplanted other gods in certain parts of the country; and an important cycle of myths was formed round him and his consort Isis.

Osiris was the son of the Sun-god, his brother was Typhon-Set, and his sister was Isis. Osiris married his sister, and together they reigned over Egypt. The wicked brother, Typhon, meditated killing Osiris. He had a chest made which was exactly the length of Osiris' body. At a banquet this chest was offered to the person whom it exactly fitted. This was Osiris and none other! He entered the chest. Typhon and his confederates rushed upon him, closed the chest, and threw it into the river. When Isis heard the terrible news she wandered far and wide in despair, seeking her husband's body. When she had found it, Typhon again took possession of it, and tore it in fourteen pieces which were dispersed in many different places. Various tombs of Osiris were shown in Egypt. In many places, up and down the country, portions of the god were said to be buried. Osiris himself, however, came forth from the nether-world and vanquished Typhon. A beam shone from him upon Isis, who in consequence bore a son, Harpocrates or Horus.

And now let us compare this myth with the view which the Greek philosopher, Empedocles (B.C. 490-430) takes of the universe. He assumes that the one original primeval being was once broken up into the four elements, fire, water, earth, and air, or into the multiplicity of being. He represents two opposing forces, which within this world of existence bring about growth and decay, love and strife. Empedocles says of the elements:

They remain ever the same, but yet by combining their forces
Become transformed into men and the numberless beings besides.
These are now joined into one, love binding the many together,
Now once again they are scattered, dispersing through hatred and strife.

What then are the things in the world from Empedocles' point of view? They are the elements in different combinations. They could only come into being because the Primeval Unity was broken up into the four essences. Therefore this primordial unity was poured into the elements. Anything confronting us is part of the divinity which was poured out. But the divinity is hidden in the thing; it first had to die that things might come into being. And what are these things? Mixtures of divine constituents effectuated by love and hatred. Empedocles says this distinctly:

See, for a clear demonstration, how the limbs of a man are constructed,
All that the body possesses, in beauty and pride of existence,
All put together by love, are the elements there forming one.
Afterwards hatred and strife come, and fatally tear them asunder,
Once more they wander alone, on the desolate confines of life.
So it is with the bushes and trees, and the water-inhabiting fishes,
Wild animals roaming the mountains, and ships swiftly borne by their sails.

Empedocles therefore must come to the conclusion that the sage finds again the Divine Primordial Unity, hidden in the world by a spell, and entangled in the meshes of love and hatred. But if man finds the divine, he must himself be divine, for Empedocles takes the point of view that a being is only cognised by its equal. This conviction of his is expressed in Goethe's lines:

"If the eye were not of the nature of the sun, how could we behold light? If divine force were not at work in us, how could divine things delight us?"

These thoughts about the world and man, which transcend sense-experience, were found by the Mystic in the myth of Osiris. Divine creative force has been poured out into the universe; it appears as the four elements; God (Osiris) is killed. Man is to raise him from the dead with his cognition, which is of divine nature. He is to find him again as Horus (the Son of God, the Logos, Wisdom), in the opposition between Strife (Typhon) and Love (Isis). Empedocles expresses his fundamental conviction in Greek form by means of images which border on myth. Love is Aphrodite, and strife is Neikos. They bind and unbind the elements.

The portrayal of the content of a myth in the manner followed here must not be confused with a merely symbolical or even allegorical interpretation of myths. This is not intended. The images forming the contents of a myth are not invented symbols of abstract truths, but actual soul-experiences of the initiate. He experiences the images with his spiritual organs of perception, just as the normal man experiences the images of physical things with his eyes and ears. But as an image is nothing in itself if it is not aroused in the perception by an outer object, so the mythical image is nothing unless it is excited by real facts of the spiritual world. Only in regard to the physical world, man is at first outside the exciting causes, whereas he can only experience the images of myths when he is within the corresponding spiritual occurrences. In order, however, to be within them, he must have gone through initiation. Then the spiritual occurrences within which he is perceiving are, as it were, illustrated by the myth-images. Any one who cannot take the mythical element as such illustration of real spiritual occurrences, has not yet attained to the understanding of it. For the spiritual events themselves are supersensible, and images which are reminiscent of the physical world are not themselves of a spiritual nature, but only an illustration of spiritual things. One who lives merely in the images lives in a dream. Only one who has got to the point of feeling the spiritual element in the image as he feels in the sense-world a rose through the image of a rose, really lives in spiritual perceptions. This is the reason why the images of myths cannot have only one meaning. On account of their illustrative character, the same myths may express several spiritual facts. It is not therefore a contradiction when interpreters of myths sometimes connect a myth with one spiritual fact and sometimes with another.

From this standpoint, we are able to find a thread to conduct us through the labyrinth of Greek myths. Let us consider the legend of Heracles. The twelve labours imposed upon Heracles appear in a higher light when we remember that before the last and most difficult one, he is initiated into the Eleusinian mysteries. He is commissioned by King Eurystheus of Mycenæ to bring the hell-hound Cerberus from the infernal regions and take it back there again. In order to undertake the descent into hell, Heracles had to be initiated. The Mysteries conducted man through the death of perishable things, therefore into the nether-world, and by initiation they rescued his eternal part from perishing. As a Mystic, he could vanquish death. Heracles having become a Mystic overcomes the dangers of the nether-world. This justifies us in interpreting his other ordeals as stages in the inner development of the soul. He overcomes the Nemæan lion and brings him to Mycenæ. This means that he becomes master of purely physical force in man; he tames it. Afterwards he slays the nine-headed Hydra. He overcomes it with firebrands and dips his arrows in its gall, so that they become deadly. This means that he overcomes lower knowledge, that which comes through the senses. He does this through the fire of the spirit, and from what he has gained through the lower knowledge, he draws the power to look at lower things in the light which belongs to spiritual sight. Heracles captures the hind of Artemis, goddess of hunting: everything which free nature offers to the human soul, Heracles conquers and subdues. The other labours may be interpreted in the same way. We cannot here trace out every detail, and only wish to describe how the general sense of the myth points to inner development.

A similar interpretation is possible of the expedition of the Argonauts. Phrixus and his sister Helle, children of a Bœotian king, suffered many things from their step-mother. The gods sent them a ram with a golden fleece, which flew away with them. When they came to the straits between Europe and Asia, Helle was drowned. Hence the strait is called the Hellespont. Phrixus came to the King of Colchis, on the east shore of the Black Sea. He sacrificed the ram to the gods, and gave its fleece to King Æetes. The king had it hung up in a grove and guarded by a terrible dragon. The Greek hero Jason undertook to fetch the fleece from Colchis, in company with other heroes, Heracles, Theseus, and Orpheus. Heavy tasks were laid upon Jason by Æetes for the obtaining of the treasure, but Medea, the king's daughter, who was versed in magic, aided him. He subdued two fire-breathing bulls. He ploughed a field and sowed in it dragon's teeth from which armed men grew up out of the earth. By Medea's advice he threw a stone into their midst, whereupon they killed each other. Jason lulls the dragon to sleep with a charm of Medea's and is then able to win the fleece. He returns with it to Greece, Medea accompanying him as his wife. The king pursues the fugitives. In order to detain him, Medea slays her little brother Absyrtus, and scatters his limbs in the sea. Æetes stays to collect them, and the pair are able to reach Jason's home with the fleece.

Each of these facts requires a deep elucidation. The fleece is something belonging to man, and infinitely precious to him. It is something from which he was separated in times of yore, and for the recovery of which he has to overcome terrible forces. It is thus with the eternal in the human soul. It belongs to man, but man is separated from it by his lower nature. Only by overcoming the latter, and lulling it to sleep, can he recover the eternal. This becomes possible when his own consciousness (Medea) comes to his aid with its magic power. Medea is to Jason what Diotima was to Socrates, a teacher of love (*cf.* p. 88). Man's own wisdom has the magic power necessary for attaining the divine after having overcome the transitory. From the lower nature there can only arise a lower human principle, the armed men who are overcome by spiritual force, the counsel of Medea. Even when man has found the eternal, the fleece, he is not yet safe. He has to sacrifice part of his consciousness (Absyrtus). This is exacted by the physical world, which we can only apprehend as a multiple (dismembered) world. We might go still deeper into the description of the spiritual events lying behind the images, but it is only intended here to indicate the principle of the formation of myths.

Of special interest, when interpreted in this way, is the legend of Prometheus. He and his brother Epimetheus are sons of the Titan Iapetus. The Titans are the offspring of the oldest generation of gods, Uranus (Heaven) and Gæa (Earth). Kronos, the youngest of the Titans, dethroned his father and seized upon the government of the world. In return, he was overpowered, with the other Titans, by his son Zeus, who became the chief of the gods. In the struggle with the Titans, Prometheus was on the side of Zeus. By his advice, Zeus banished the Titans to the nether-world. But in Prometheus there still lived the Titan spirit, he was only half a friend to Zeus. When the latter wished to exterminate men on account of their arrogance, Prometheus espoused their cause, taught them numbers, writing, and everything else which leads to culture, especially the use of fire. This aroused the wrath of Zeus against Prometheus. Hephaistos, the son of Zeus, was commissioned to make a female form of great beauty, whom the gods adorned with every possible gift. She was called Pandora, the all-gifted one. Hermes, messenger of the gods, brought her to Epimetheus, the brother of Prometheus. She brought him a casket, as a present from the gods. Epimetheus accepted the present, although Prometheus had warned him against receiving any gift from the gods. When the casket was opened, every possible human evil flew out of it. Hope alone remained, and this because Pandora quickly closed the box. Hope has therefore been left to man, as a doubtful gift of the gods. By order of Zeus, Prometheus was chained to a rock on the Caucasus, on account of his relation to man. An eagle perpetually gnaws his liver, which is as often renewed. He has to pass his life in agonising loneliness till one of the gods voluntarily sacrifices himself, *i.e.*, devotes himself to death. The tormented Prometheus bears his sufferings steadfastly. It had been told him that Zeus would be dethroned by the son of a mortal unless Zeus consented to wed this mortal woman. It was important for Zeus to know this secret.

He sent the messenger Hermes to Prometheus, in order to learn something about it. Prometheus refused to say anything. The legend of Heracles is connected with that of Prometheus. In the course of his wanderings Heracles comes to the Caucasus. He slays the eagle which was devouring the liver of Prometheus. The centaur Chiron, who cannot die, although suffering from an incurable wound, sacrifices himself for Prometheus, who is thereupon reconciled with the gods.

The Titans are the force of will, proceeding as nature (Kronos) from the original universal spirit (Uranus). Here we have to think not merely of will-forces in an abstract form, but of actual will-beings. Prometheus is one of them, and this describes his nature. But he is not altogether a Titan. In a certain sense he is on the side of Zeus, the Spirit, who enters upon the rulership of the world after the unbridled force of nature (Kronos) has been subdued. Prometheus is thus the representative of those worlds which have given man the progressive element, half nature-force, half spiritual force, man's will. The will points on the one side towards good, on the other, towards evil. Its fate is decided according as it leans to the spiritual or the perishable. This fate is that of man himself. He is chained to the perishable, the eagle gnaws him, he has to suffer. He can only reach the highest by seeking his destiny in solitude. He has a secret which is that the divine (Zeus) must marry a mortal (human consciousness bound up with the physical body), in order to beget a son, human wisdom (the Logos) which will deliver the deity. By this means consciousness becomes immortal. He must not betray this secret till a Mystic (Heracles) comes to him, and annihilates the power which was perpetually threatening him with death. A being half animal, half human, a centaur, is obliged to sacrifice itself to redeem man. The centaur is man himself, half animal, half spiritual. He must die in order that the purely spiritual man may be delivered. That which is disdained by Prometheus, human will, is accepted by Epimetheus, reason or prudence. But the gifts offered to Epimetheus are only troubles and sorrows, for reason clings to the transitory and perishable. And only one thing is left—the hope that even out of the perishable the eternal may some day be born.

The thread running through the legends of the Argonauts, Heracles and Prometheus, is continued in Homer's *Odyssey*. Here we find ourselves compelled to use our own method of interpretation. But on closer consideration of everything which has to be taken into account, even the sturdiest doubter must lose all scruples about such an interpretation. In the first place, it is a startling fact that it is also related of Odysseus that he descended into the nether-world. Whatever we may think about the author of the *Odyssey* in other respects, it is impossible to imagine his representing a mortal descending to the infernal regions, without his bringing him into connection with what the journey into the nether-world meant to the Greeks.

It meant the conquest of the perishable and the awakening of the eternal in the soul. It must therefore be conceded that Odysseus accomplished this, and thereby his experiences and those of Heracles acquire a deeper significance. They become a delineation of the non-sensuous, of the soul's progress of development. Hence the narrative in the *Odyssey* is different from what is demanded by a history of outer events. The hero makes voyages in enchanted ships. Actual geographical distances are dealt with in most arbitrary fashion. It is not in the least a question of what is physically real. This becomes comprehensible, if the physically real events are only related for the sake of illustrating the development of a soul. Moreover the poet himself at the opening of the book says that it deals with a search for the soul:

"O Muse, sing to me of the man full of resource, who wandered very much after he had destroyed the sacred city of Troy, and saw the cities of many men, and learned their manners. Many griefs also in his mind did he suffer on the sea, although seeking to preserve his own soul, and the return of his companions."

We have before us a man seeking for the soul, for the divine, and his wanderings during this search are narrated. He comes to the land of the Cyclopes. These are uncouth giants, with only one eye and that in the centre of the forehead. The most terrible, Polyphemus, devours several of Odysseus' companions. Odysseus himself escapes by blinding the Cyclopes. Here we have to do with the first stage of life's pilgrimage. Physical force or the lower nature has to be overcome. It devours any one who does not take away its power, who does not blind it. Odysseus next comes to the island of the enchantress Circe. She changes some of his companions into grunting pigs. She also is subdued by Odysseus. Circe is the lower mind-force, which cleaves to the transitory. If misused, it may thrust men down even deeper into bestiality. Odysseus has to overcome it. Then he is able to descend into the nether-world. He becomes a Mystic. Now he is exposed to the dangers which beset the Mystic on his progress from the lower to the higher degrees of initiation. He comes to the Sirens, who lure the passer-by to death by sweet magic sounds. These are the forms of the lower imagination, which are at first pursued by one who has freed himself from the power of the senses. He has got so far that his spirit acts freely, but is not initiated. He pursues illusions, from the power of which he must break loose. Odysseus has to accomplish the awful passage between Scylla and Charybdis. The Mystic, at the beginning of the path wavers between spirit and sensuousness. He cannot yet grasp the full value of spirit, yet sensuousness has already lost its former attraction. All Odysseus' companions perish in a shipwreck; he alone escapes and comes to the nymph Calypso, who receives him kindly and takes care of him for seven years. At length, by order of Zeus, she dismisses him to his home. The Mystic has arrived at a stage at which all his fellow-aspirants fail; he alone, Odysseus, is worthy. He enjoys for a time, which is defined by the mystically symbolic number seven, the rest of gradual initiation. Before Odysseus arrives at his home, he comes to the isle of the Phæaces, where he meets with a hospitable reception. The king's daughter gives him sympathy, and the king, Alcinous, entertains and honours him. Once more does Odysseus approach the world and its joys, and the spirit which is attached to the world, Nausicaa, awakes within him. But he finds the way home, to the divine. At first nothing good awaits him at home. His wife, Penelope, is surrounded by numerous suitors. Each one she promises to marry, when she has finished weaving a certain piece of work. She avoids keeping her promise by undoing every night what she has woven by day. Odysseus is obliged to vanquish the suitors before he can be reunited to his wife in peace. The goddess Athene changes him into a beggar so that he may not be recognised at his entrance; and thus he overcomes the suitors. Odysseus is seeking his own deeper consciousness, the divine powers of the soul. He wishes to be united with them. Before the Mystic can find them, he must overcome everything which sues for the favour of that consciousness. The band of suitors spring from the world of lower reality, from perishable nature. The logic directed against them is a spinning which is always undone again after it has been spun. Wisdom (the goddess Athene) is the sure guide to the deepest powers of the soul. It changes man into a beggar, *i.e.*, it divests him of everything of a transitory nature.

The Eleusinian festivals, which were celebrated in Greece in honour of Demeter and Dionysos, were steeped in the wisdom of the Mysteries. A sacred road led from Athens to Eleusis. It was bordered with mysterious signs, intended to bring the soul into an exalted mood. In Eleusis were mysterious temples, served by families of priests. The dignity and the wisdom which was bound up with it were inherited in these families from generation to generation. (Instructive information about the organisation of these sanctuaries will be found in Karl Bötticher's *Ergänzungen zu den letzten Untersuchungen auf der Akropolis in Athen*, Philologus, Supplement, vol. iii, part 3.) The wisdom, which qualified for the priesthood, was the wisdom of the Greek Mysteries. The festivals, which were celebrated twice a year, represented the great world-drama of the destiny of the divine in the world, and of that of the human soul. The lesser Mysteries took place in February, the greater in September. Initiations were connected with the festivals. The symbolical presentation of the cosmic and human drama formed the final act of the initiations of the Mystics, which took place here.

The Eleusinian temples had been erected in honour of the goddess Demeter. She was a daughter of Kronos. She had given to Zeus a daughter,

Persephone, before his marriage with Hera. Persephone, while playing, was carried away by Hades (Pluto), the god of the infernal regions. Demeter wandered far and wide over the earth, seeking her with lamentations. Sitting on a stone in Eleusis, she was found by the daughters of Keleus, ruler of the place; in the form of an old woman she entered the service of his family, as nurse to the queen's son. She wished to endow this boy with immortality, and for this purpose hid him in fire every night. When his mother discovered this, she wept and lamented. After that the bestowal of immortality was impossible. Demeter left the house. Keleus then built a temple. The grief of Demeter for Persephone was limitless. She spread sterility over the earth. The gods had to appease her, to prevent a great catastrophe. Then Zeus induced Hades (Pluto) to release Persephone into the upper world, but before letting her go, he gave her a pomegranate to eat. This obliged her to return periodically to the nether-world for evermore. Henceforward she spent a third of the year there, and two-thirds in the world above. Demeter was appeased and returned to Olympus; but at Eleusis, the place of her suffering, she founded the cult which should keep her fate in remembrance.

It is not difficult to discover the meaning of the myth of Demeter and Persephone. It is the soul which lives alternately above and below. The immortality of the soul and its perpetually recurring transformation by birth and death are thus symbolised. The soul originates from the immortal—Demeter. But it is led astray by the transitory, and even prevailed upon to share its destiny. It has partaken of the fruits in the nether-world, the human soul is satisfied with the transitory, therefore it cannot permanently live in the heights of the divine. It has always to return to the realm of the perishable. Demeter is the representative of the essence from which human consciousness arose; but we must think of it as the consciousness which was able to come into being through the spiritual forces of the earth. Thus Demeter is the primordial essence of the earth, and the endowment of the earth with the seed-forces of the produce of the fields through her, points to a still deeper side of her being. This being wishes to give man immortality. She hides her nursling in fire by night. But man cannot bear the pure force of fire (the spirit). Demeter is obliged to abandon the idea. She is only able to found a temple service, through which man is able to participate in the divine as far as this is possible.

The Eleusinian festivals were an eloquent confession of the belief in the immortality of the human soul. This confession found symbolic expression in the Persephone myth. Together with Demeter and Persephone Dionysos was commemorated in Eleusis. As Demeter was honoured as the divine creatress of the eternal in man, so in Dionysos was honoured the ever-changing divine in the world. The divine poured into the world and torn to pieces in order to be spiritually reborn (*cf.* p. 90) had to be honoured together with Demeter. (A brilliant description of the spirit of the Eleusinian Mysteries is found in Edouard Schuré's book, *Sanctuaires d'Orient*. Paris, 1898.)

VI

THE MYSTERY WISDOM OF EGYPT

When leaving thy body behind thee, thou soarest into the ether,
Then thou becomest a god, immortal, not subject to death.

In this utterance of Empedocles (*cf.* p. 55) is epitomised what the ancient Egyptians thought about the eternal element in man and its connection with the divine. The proof of this may be found in the so-called *Book of the Dead*, which has been deciphered by the diligence of nineteenth-century investigators (*cf.* Lepsius, *Das Totenbuch der alten Ägypter*, Berlin, 1842). It is "the greatest continuous literary work which has come down to us from ancient Egypt." All kinds of instructions and prayers are contained in it, which were put into the tomb of each deceased person to serve as a guide when he was released from his mortal tenement. The most intimate ideas of the Egyptians about the Eternal and the origin of the world are contained in this work. These ideas point to a conception of the gods similar to that of Greek mysticism.

Osiris gradually became the favourite and most universally recognised of the various deities worshipped in different parts of Egypt. In him were comprised the ideas about the other divinities. Whatever the majority of the Egyptian people may have thought about Osiris, the *Book of the Dead* indicates that the priestly wisdom saw in him a being that might be found in the human soul itself. Everything said about death and the dead shows this plainly. While the body is given to earth, and kept by it, the eternal part of man enters upon the path to the primordial eternal. It comes before the tribunal of Osiris, and the forty-two judges of the dead. The fate of the eternal part of man depends on the verdict of these judges. If the soul has confessed its sins and been deemed reconciled to eternal justice, invisible powers approach it and say: "The Osiris N. has been purified in the pool which is south of the field of Hotep and north of the field of Locusts, where the gods of verdure purify themselves at the fourth hour of the night and the eighth hour of the day with the image of the heart of the gods, passing from night to day." Thus, within the eternal cosmic order, the eternal part of man is addressed as an Osiris. After the name Osiris comes the deceased person's own name. And the one who is being united with the eternal cosmic order also calls himself "Osiris." "I am the Osiris N. Growing under the blossoms of the fig-tree is the name of the Osiris N." Man therefore becomes an Osiris. Being Osiris is only a perfect stage in human development. It seems obvious that even the Osiris who is a judge within the eternal cosmic order is nothing else but a perfect man. Between being human and divine, there is a difference in degree and number. The mystic view of the mystery of "number" underlies this. Osiris as a cosmic being is One, yet on this account he exists undivided in each human soul. Each person is an Osiris, yet the One Osiris must be represented as a separate being. Man is in course of development; at the end of his evolutionary career, he becomes divine. In taking this view, we must speak of divinity, or becoming divine, rather than of a separate divine being, complete in himself.

It cannot be doubted but that according to this view only he can really enter upon the Osiris existence, who has reached the portals of the eternal cosmic order as an Osiris. Thus, the highest life which man can lead must consist in his changing himself into Osiris. Even during mortal life, a true man will live as a perfect Osiris as far as he can. He becomes perfect when he lives as an Osiris, when he passes through the experiences of Osiris. In this way, we see the deeper significance of the Osiris myth. It becomes the ideal of the man who wishes to awaken the eternal within him.

Osiris is torn to pieces and killed by Typhon. The fragments of his body are preserved and cared for by his consort, Isis. After his death he let a ray of his own light fall upon her, and she bore him Horus. This Horus takes up the earthly tasks of Osiris. He is the second Osiris, still imperfect, but progressing towards the true Osiris.

The true Osiris is in the human soul, which at first is of a transitory nature; but as such, it is destined to give birth to the eternal. Man may, therefore, regard himself as the tomb of Osiris. The lower nature (Typhon) has killed the higher nature in him. Love in his soul (Isis) must take care of the dead fragments of his body, and then the higher nature, the eternal soul (Horus) will be born, which can progress to Osiris life. The man who is aspiring to the highest kind of existence must repeat in himself, as a microcosm, the macrocosmic universal Osiris process. This is the meaning of Egyptian initiation. What Plato (*cf.* p. 80) describes as a cosmic process, *i.e.*, that the Creator has stretched the soul of the world on the body of the world in the form of a cross, and that the cosmic process is the release of this crucified soul,—this process had to be enacted in man on a smaller scale if he was to be qualified for Osiris life. The candidate for initiation had to develop himself in such a way that his soul-experience, his becoming an Osiris, became blended into one with the cosmic Osiris process.

If we could look into the temples of initiation in which people underwent the transformation into Osiris, we should see that what took place represented microcosmically the building of the cosmos. Man who proceeded from the "Father" was to give birth to the Son in himself. What he actually bears within him, divinity hidden under a spell, was to become manifest in him. This divinity is kept down in him by the power of the earthly nature; this lower nature must first be buried in order that the higher nature may arise.

From this we are able to interpret what we are told about the incidents of initiation. The candidate was subjected to mysterious processes, by means of which his earthly nature was killed, and his higher part awakened. It is not necessary to study these processes in detail, if we understand their meaning. This meaning is contained in the confession possible to every one who went through initiation. He could say: "Before me was the endless perspective at the end of which is the perfection of the divine. I felt that the power of the divine is within me. I buried what in me keeps down that power. I died to earthly things. I was dead. I had died as a lower man, I was in the nether-world. I had intercourse with the dead, *i.e.*, with those who have already become part of the chain of the eternal cosmic order. After my sojourn in the nether-world, I arose from the dead. I overcame death, but now I have become different. I have nothing more to do with perishable nature. It has in me become saturated with the Logos. I now belong to those who live eternally, and who will sit at the right hand of Osiris. I myself shall be a true Osiris, part of the eternal cosmic order, and judgment of life and death will be placed in my hands." The candidate for initiation had to submit to the experience which made such a confession possible to him. Thus this was an experience of the highest kind.

Let us now imagine that a non-initiate hears of such experiences. He cannot know what has really taken place in the initiate's soul. In his eyes, the initiate died physically, lay in the grave, and rose again. What is a spiritual reality at a higher stage of existence appears when expressed in the form of sense-reality as an event which breaks through the order of nature. It is a "miracle." So far initiation was a miracle. One who really wished to understand it must have awakened within him powers to enable him to stand on a higher plane of existence. He must have approached these higher experiences through a course of life specially adapted for the purpose. In whatever way these prepared experiences were enacted in individual cases, they are always found to be of quite a definite type. And so an initiate's life is a typical one. It may be described independently of the single personality. Or rather, an individual could only be described as being on the way to the divine if he had passed through these definite typical experiences.

Such a personality was Buddha, living in the midst of his disciples. As such an one did Jesus appear to his community. Nowadays we know of the parallelism that exists between the biographies of Buddha and of Jesus. Rudolf Seydel has convincingly proved this parallelism in his book, *Buddha und Christus*. (Compare also the excellent essay by Dr. Hübbe-Schleiden,

"Jesus ein Buddhist.") We have only to follow out the two lives in detail in order to see that all objections to the parallelism are futile.

The birth of Buddha is announced by a white elephant, which descends from heaven and declares to the queen, Maya, that she will bring forth a divine man, who "will attune all beings to love and friendship, and will unite them in a close alliance." We read in St. Luke's Gospel: "To a virgin espoused to a man whose name was Joseph, of the house of David; and the virgin's name was Mary. And the angel came in unto her, and said, 'Hail, thou that art highly favoured.... Behold, thou shalt conceive in thy womb, and bring forth a son, and shalt call his name Jesus. He shall be great, and shall be called the Son of the Highest.'"

The Brahmins, or Indian priests, who know what the birth of a Buddha means, interpret Maya's dream. They have a definite, typical idea of a Buddha, to which the life of the personality about to be born will have to correspond. Similarly we read in Matthew ii. *et seq.*, that when Herod "had gathered all the chief priests and scribes of the people together, he demanded of them where Christ should be born." The Brahmin Asita says of Buddha: "This is the child which will become Buddha, the redeemer, the leader to immortality, freedom, and light." Compare with this Luke ii. 25: "And, behold, there was a man in Jerusalem, whose name was Simeon; and the same man was just and devout, waiting for the consolation of Israel: and the Holy Ghost was upon him.... And when the parents brought in the child Jesus, to do for him after the custom of the law, then took he him up in his arms, and blessed God, and said, Lord, now lettest thou thy servant depart in peace, according to thy word: for mine eyes have seen thy salvation, which thou hast prepared before the face of all people; a light to lighten the Gentiles, and the glory of thy people Israel."

It is related of Buddha that at the age of twelve he was lost, and found again under a tree, surrounded by poets and sages of the olden time, whom he was teaching. With this incident the following passage in St. Luke corresponds: "Now his parents went to Jerusalem every year at the feast of the passover. And when he was twelve years old, they went up to Jerusalem after the custom of the feast. And when they had fulfilled the days, as they returned, the child Jesus tarried behind in Jerusalem; and Joseph and his mother knew not of it. But they, supposing him to have been in the company, went a day's journey; and they sought him among their kinsfolk and acquaintance. And when they found him not, they turned back again to Jerusalem, seeking him. And it came to pass that after three days they found him in the temple, sitting in the midst of the doctors, both hearing them, and asking them questions. And all that heard him were astonished at his understanding and answers" (Luke ii. 41-47).

After Buddha had lived in solitude, and returned, he was received by the benediction of a virgin, "Blessed is thy mother, blessed is thy father, blessed is the wife to whom thou belongest." But he replied, "Only they are blessed who are in Nirvana," *i.e.*, who have entered the eternal cosmic order. In St. Luke's Gospel (xi. 27), we read: "And it came to pass, as he spake these things, a certain woman of the company lifted up her voice and said unto him, 'Blessed is the womb that bare thee, and the paps which thou hast sucked.' But he said, 'Yea rather, blessed are they that hear the word of God, and keep it.'"

In the course of Buddha's life, the tempter comes to him and promises him all the kingdoms of the earth. Buddha refuses everything in the words: "I know well that I am destined to have a kingdom, but I do not desire an earthly one. I shall become Buddha and make all the world exult with joy." The tempter has to own that his reign is over. Jesus answers the same temptation in the words: "Get thee hence, Satan, for it is written, Thou shalt worship the Lord thy God, and him only shalt thou serve. Then the devil leaveth him" (Matthew iv. 10, 11). This description of the parallelism might be extended to many other points with the same result.

The life of Buddha ended sublimely. On a journey, he felt ill; he came to the river Hiranja, near Kuschinagara. There he lay down on a carpet which his favourite disciple, Ananda, spread for him. His body began to be luminous from within. He died transfigured, his body irradiating light, saying, "Nothing endures."

The death of Buddha corresponds with the transfiguration of Jesus. "And it came to pass about eight days after these sayings, he took Peter and John and James, and went up into a mountain to pray. And as he prayed, the fashion of his countenance was altered, and his raiment was white and glistering."

Buddha's earthly life ends at this point, but it is here that the most important part of the life of Jesus begins,—His suffering, death, and resurrection. Other accounts of Buddha's death need not here be considered, even though they reveal profound aspects.

The agreement in these two redemptive lives leads to the same conclusion. The narratives themselves indicate the nature of this conclusion. When the priest-sages hear what kind of birth is to take place, they know what is involved. They know that they have to do with a Divine man; they know beforehand what kind of personality it is who is appearing. And therefore his course of life can only correspond with what they know about the life of a Divine man. In the wisdom of their Mysteries such a life is traced out for all eternity. It *can* only be as it *must* be; it comes into manifestation like an eternal law of nature. Just as a chemical substance can only behave in a certain definite way, so a Buddha or a Christ can only live in a certain definite way.

His life is not described merely by writing a casual biography; it is much better described by giving the typical features which are contained for all time in the wisdom of the Mysteries. The Buddha legend is no more a biography in the ordinary sense than the Gospels are meant to be a biography in the ordinary sense of the Christ Jesus. In neither is the merely accidental given; both relate the course of life marked out for a world-redeemer. The source of the two accounts is to be found in the mystery traditions and not in outer physical history. Jesus and Buddha are, to those who have recognised their Divine nature, initiates in the most eminent sense. Hence their lives are lifted out of things transitory, and what is known about initiates applies to them.[4] The casual incidents in their lives are not narrated. Of such it might be announced "In the beginning was the Word, and the Word was with God, and the Word was a God and the Word was made flesh and dwelt among us."

But the life of Jesus contains more than that of Buddha. Buddha's ends with the Transfiguration; the most momentous part of the life of Jesus begins after the Transfiguration. In the language of initiates this means that Buddha reached the point at which divine light begins to shine in men. He faces mortal death. He becomes the light of the world. Jesus goes farther. He does not physically die at the moment when the light of the world shines through him. At that moment he is a Buddha. But at that very moment he enters upon a stage which finds expression in a higher degree of initiation. He suffers and dies. What is earthly disappears. But the spiritual element, the light of the world, does not. His resurrection follows. He is revealed to his followers as Christ. Buddha, at the moment of his Transfiguration, flows into the blissful life of the Universal Spirit. Christ Jesus awakens the Universal Spirit once more, but in a human form, in present existence. Such an event had formerly taken place at the higher stages of initiation. Those initiated in the spirit of the Osiris myth attained to such a resurrection. In the life of Jesus, this "great" initiation was added to the Buddha initiation. Buddha demonstrated by his life that man is the Logos, and that he returns to the Logos, to the light, when his earthly part dies. In Jesus, the Logos himself became a person. In him, the Word was made flesh.

Therefore, what was enacted in the innermost recesses of the temples by the guardians of the ancient Mysteries has been apprehended, through Christianity, as a historical fact. The followers of Christ Jesus confessed their belief in Him, the initiate, of unique and supreme greatness. He proved to them that the world is divine. In the Christian community, the wisdom of the Mysteries was indissolubly bound up with the personality of Christ Jesus. That which man previously had sought to attain through the Mysteries was now replaced by the belief that Christ had lived on earth, and that the faithful belonged to him.

Henceforward, part of what was formerly only to be gained through mystical methods, could be replaced, in the Christian community, by the conviction that the divine had been manifested in the Word present amongst them. Not that for which each individual soul underwent a long preparation was now decisive, but what those had heard and seen who were with Jesus, and what was handed down by them. "That which was from the beginning, which we have heard, which ... our hands have handled, of the Word of life ... that which we have seen and heard declare we unto you, that ye also may have fellowship with us." Thus do we read in the first Epistle of St. John. And this immediate reality is to embrace all future generations in a living bond of union, and as a church is mystically to extend from race to race. It is in this sense that the words of St. Augustine are to be understood, "I should not believe the Gospels unless the authority of the Catholic Church induced me to do so." Thus the Gospels do not contain within themselves testimony to their truth, but they are to be believed because they are founded on the personality of Jesus, and because the Church from that personality mysteriously draws the power to make the truth of the Gospels manifest.

The Mysteries handed down traditionally the means of arriving at truth; the Christian community itself propagates the truth. To the confidence in the mystical forces which spring up in the inmost being of man, during initiation, was added the confidence in the One, primordial Initiator.

The Mystics sought to become divine, they wished to experience divinity. Jesus was divine, we must hold fast to Him, and then we shall become partakers of His divinity, in the community founded by Him; this became Christian conviction. What became divine in Jesus was made so for all His followers. "Lo, I am with you alway, even unto the end of the world." The one who was born in Bethlehem has an eternal character independent of time. The Christmas anthem thus speaks of the birth of Jesus, as if it took place each Christmas, "Christ is born to-day, the Saviour has come into the world to-day, to-day the angels are singing on earth."

In the Christ-experience is to be seen a definite stage of initiation. When the Mystic of pre-Christian times passed through this Christ-experience, he was, through his initiation, in a state which enabled him to perceive something spiritually,—in higher worlds,—to which no fact in the world of sense corresponded. He experienced that which surrounds the Mystery of Golgotha in the higher world. If the Christian Mystic goes through this experience by initiation, he at the same time beholds the historical event which took place on Golgotha, and knows that in that event, enacted within the physical world, there is the same content as was formerly only in the supersensible facts of the Mysteries. Thus there was poured out on the Christian community, through the "Mysteries of Golgotha," that which formerly had been poured out on the Mystics within the temples. And initiation gives Christian Mystics the possibility of becoming conscious of what is contained in the "Mystery of Golgotha," whereas faith makes man an unconscious partaker of the mystical stream which flowed from the events depicted in the New Testament, and which has ever since been pervading the spiritual life of humanity.

FOOTNOTES:

[4] The great initiates raised themselves through initiation up into the sphere of the Logos and carried this Logos influence with them in their human life. The fundamental difference between them and Jesus was the fact that the Logos in the course of its evolution individualised itself into One Divine Individuality who descended into Jesus of Nazareth at the Baptism, and so that the Logos manifested its whole Divine individuality through the personality of Jesus as far as it was possible to express Divinity by human means. Such was the unique character of the Christ Jesus.

VII

THE GOSPELS

The accounts of the life of Jesus which can be submitted to historical examination are contained in the Gospels. All that does not come from this source might, in the opinion of one of those who are considered the greatest historical authorities on the subject (Harnack), be "easily written on a quarto page."

But what kind of documents are these Gospels? The fourth, that of St. John, differs so much from the others, that those who think themselves obliged to follow the path of historical research in order to study the subject, come to the conclusion: "If John possesses the genuine tradition about the life of Jesus, that of the first three Evangelists (the Synoptists) is untenable. If the Synoptists are right, the Fourth Gospel must be rejected as a historical source" (Otto Schmiedel, *Die Hauptprobleme der Leben Jesu Forschung*, p. 15). This is a statement made from the standpoint of the historical investigator.

In the present work, in which we are dealing with the mystical contents of the Gospels, such a point of view is neither to be accepted nor rejected. But attention must certainly be drawn to such an opinion as the following: "Measured by the standard of consistency, inspiration, and completeness, these writings leave very much to be desired, and even measured by the ordinary human standard, they suffer from not a few imperfections." This is the opinion of a Christian theologian (Harnack, *Wesen des Christentums*).

One who takes his stand on a mystical origin of the Gospels easily finds an explanation of what is apparently contradictory, and also discovers harmony between the fourth Gospel and the three others. For none of these writings are meant to be mere historical tradition in the ordinary sense of the word. They do not profess to give a historical biography (*cf.* p. 140 *et seq.*). What they intended to give was already shadowed forth in the traditions of the Mysteries, as the typical life of a Son of God. It was these traditions which were drawn upon, not history. Now it was only natural that these traditions should not be in complete verbal agreement in every Mystery centre. Still, the agreement was so close that the Buddhists narrated the life of their divine man almost in the same way in which the Evangelists narrated the life of Christ. But naturally there were differences. We have only to assume that the four Evangelists drew from four different mystery traditions. It testifies to the extraordinary personality of Jesus that in four writers, belonging to different traditions, he awakened the belief that he was one who so perfectly corresponded with their type of an initiate, that they were able to describe him as one who lived the typical life marked out in their Mysteries. They each described his life according to their own mystic traditions. And if the narratives of the first three Evangelists resemble each other, it proves nothing more than that they drew from similar mystery traditions. The fourth Evangelist saturated his Gospel with ideas which are, in many respects, reminiscent of the religious philosopher, Philo (*cf.* p. 82). This only proves that he was rooted in the same mystic tradition as Philo.

There are various elements in the Gospels. Firstly, facts are related, which seem to lay claim to being historical. Secondly, there are parables, in which the narrative form is only used to symbolise a deeper truth. And, thirdly, there are teachings characteristic of the Christian conception of life. In St. John's Gospel there is no real parable. The source from which he drew was a mystical school which considered parables unnecessary.

The part played by ostensibly historical facts and parables in the first three Gospels is clearly shown in the narrative of the cursing of the fig tree. In St. Mark xi. 11-14, we read: "And Jesus entered into Jerusalem, and into the temple: and when he had looked round about upon all things, and now the eventide was come, he went out unto Bethany with the twelve. And on the morrow, when they were come from Bethany, he was hungry: and seeing a fig tree afar off having leaves, he came, if haply he might find any thing thereon: and when he came to it, he found nothing but leaves; for the time of figs was not yet. And Jesus answered and said unto it, No man eat fruit of thee hereafter for ever." In the corresponding passage in St. Luke's Gospel, he relates a parable (xiii. 6, 7): "He spake also this parable; A certain man had a fig tree planted in his vineyard; and he came and sought fruit thereon, and found none. Then said he unto the dresser of his vineyard, Behold these three years I come seeking fruit on this fig tree, and find none: cut it down; why cumbereth it the ground?" This is a parable symbolising the uselessness of the old teaching, represented by the barren fig tree. That which is meant metaphorically, St. Mark relates as a fact appearing to be historical. We may therefore assume that, in general, facts related in the Gospels are not to be taken as only historical, or as if they were only to hold good in the physical world, but as mystical facts; as experiences, for the recognition of which spiritual vision is necessary, and which arise from various mystical traditions. If we admit this, the difference between the Gospel of St. John and the Synoptists ceases to exist. For mystical interpretation, historical research has not to be taken into account. Even if one or another Gospel were written a few decades earlier or later than the others, they are all of like historical value to the mystic, St. John's Gospel as well as the others.

And the "miracles" do not present the least difficulty when interpreted mystically. They are supposed to break through the laws of nature. They only do this when they are considered as events which have so come about on the physical plane, in the perishable world, that ordinary sense-perception could see through them offhand. But if they are experiences which can only be fathomed on a higher stage of existence, namely the spiritual, it is obvious that they cannot be understood by means of the laws of physical nature.

It is thus first of all necessary to read the Gospels correctly; then we shall know in what way they are speaking of the Founder of Christianity. Their intention is to relate his life in the manner in which communications were made through the Mysteries. They relate it in the way in which a Mystic would speak of an initiate. Only, they give the initiation as the unique characteristic of one unique being. And they make salvation depend on man's holding fast to the initiate of this unique order. What had come to the initiates was the "kingdom of God." This unique being has brought the kingdom to all who will cleave to him. What was formerly the personal concern of each individual has become the common concern of all those who are willing to acknowledge Jesus as their Lord.

We can understand how this came about if we admit that the wisdom of the Mysteries was imbedded in the popular religion of the Jews. Christianity arose out of Judaism. We need not therefore be surprised at finding engrafted on Judaism, together with Christianity those mystical ideas which we have seen to be the common property of Greek and Egyptian spiritual life. If we examine national religions, we find various conceptions of the spiritual; but if, in each case, we go back to the deeper wisdom of the priests, which proves to be the spiritual nucleus of them all, we find agreement everywhere. Plato knows himself to be in agreement with the priest-sages of Egypt when he is trying to set forth the main content of Greek wisdom in his philosophical view of the universe. It is related of Pythagoras that he travelled to Egypt and India, and was instructed by the sages in those countries. Thinkers who lived in the earlier days of Christianity found so much agreement between the philosophical teachings of Plato and the deeper meaning of the Mosaic writings, that they called Plato a Moses with Attic tongue.

Thus Mystery wisdom existed everywhere. In Judaism it acquired a form which it had to assume if it was to become a world-religion.

Judaism expected the Messiah. It is not to be wondered at that when the personality of an unique initiate appeared, the Jews could only conceive of him as being the Messiah. Indeed this circumstance throws light on the fact that what had been an individual matter in the Mysteries became an affair of the whole nation. The Jewish religion had from the beginning been a national religion. The Jewish people looked upon itself as one organism. Its Jao was the God of the whole nation. If the son of this God were to be born, he must be the redeemer of the whole nation. The individual Mystic was not to be saved apart from others, the whole nation was to share in the redemption.

That one is to die for all is founded on the fundamental ideas of the Jewish religion.

It is also certain that there were mysteries in Judaism, which could be brought out of the dimness of a secret cult into the popular religion. A fully-developed mysticism existed side by side with the priestly wisdom which was attached to the outer formalism of the Pharisees. This mystery wisdom is spoken of among the Jews just as it is elsewhere. When one day an initiate was speaking of it, and his hearers sensed the secret meaning of his words, they said: "Old man, what hast thou done? Oh, that thou hadst kept silence! Thou thinkest to navigate the boundless ocean without sail or mast. This is what thou art attempting. Wilt thou fly upwards? Thou canst not. Wilt thou descend into the depths? An immeasurable abyss is yawning before thee." And the Kabbalists, from whom the above is taken, also speak of four Rabbis; and these four Rabbis sought the secret path to the divine. The first died; the second lost his reason; the third caused monstrous evils, and only the fourth, Rabbi Akiba, went in and out of the spiritual world in peace.

We thus see that within Judaism also there was a soil in which an initiate of an unique kind could develop. He had only to say to himself: "I will not let salvation be limited to a few chosen people. I will let all people participate in it." He was to carry out into the world at large what the elect had experienced in the temples of the Mysteries. He had to be willing to take upon himself to be, in spirit, to his community, through his personality, that which the cult of the Mysteries had heretofore been to those who took part in them. It is true he could not at once give to the whole community the experiences of the Mysteries, nor would he have wished to do so. But he wished to give to all the certainty of the truth contemplated in the Mysteries. He wished to cause the life, which flowed within the Mysteries, to flow through the further historical evolution of humanity, and thus to raise mankind to a higher stage of existence. "Blessed are they that have not seen, and yet have believed." He wished to plant unshakably in human hearts, in the form of confidence, the certainty that the divine really exists. One who stands outside initiation and has this confidence will certainly go further than one who is without it. It must have weighed like a mountain on the mind of Jesus to think that there might be many standing outside who do not find the way. He wished to lessen the gulf between those to be initiated and the "people." Christianity was to be a means by which every one might find the way. Should one or another not yet be ripe, at any rate he is not cut off from the possibility of sharing, more or less unconsciously, in the benefit of the spiritual current flowing through the Mysteries. "The Son of Man is come to seek and to save that which was lost." Henceforward even those who cannot yet share in initiation may enjoy some of the fruits of the Mysteries. Henceforth the Kingdom of God was not to be dependent on outward ceremonies: "Neither shall they say, Lo here! or, Lo there! for, behold, the Kingdom of God is within you." With Jesus the point in question was not so much how far this or that person advanced in the kingdom of the spirit, as that all should be convinced that that kingdom exists. "In this rejoice not, that the spirits are subject unto you; but rather rejoice, because your names are written in heaven." That is, have confidence in the divine. The time will come when you will find it.

VIII

THE LAZARUS MIRACLE

Amongst the "miracles" attributed to Jesus, very special importance must be attached to the raising of Lazarus at Bethany. Everything combines to assign a prominent position in the New Testament to that which is here related by the Evangelist. We must bear in mind that St. John alone relates it, the Evangelist who by the weighty words with which he opens his Gospel claims for it a very definite interpretation.

St. John begins with these sentences: "In the beginning was the Word, and the Word was with God, and the word was a God.... And the Word was made flesh, and dwelt among us, and we beheld his glory, a glory as of the only begotten of the Father, full of grace and truth."

One who places such words at the beginning of his narrative is plainly indicating that he wishes it to be interpreted in a very deep sense. The man who approaches it with merely intellectual explanations, or otherwise in a superficial way, is like one who thinks that Othello on the stage really murders Desdemona. What then is it that St. John means to say in his introductory words? He plainly says that he is speaking of something eternal, which existed at the beginning of things. He relates facts, but they are not to be taken as facts observed by the eye and ear, and upon which logical reason exercises its skill. He hides behind facts the "Word" which is in the Cosmic Spirit. For him, the facts are the medium in which a higher meaning is expressed. And we may therefore assume that in the fact of a man being raised from the dead, a fact which offers the greatest difficulties to the eye, ear, and logical reason, the very deepest meaning lies concealed.

Another thing has to be taken into consideration. Renan, in his *Life of Jesus*, has pointed out that the raising of Lazarus undoubtedly had a decisive influence on the end of the life of Jesus. Such a thought appears impossible from the point of view which Renan takes. For why should the fact that the belief was being circulated amongst the populace that Jesus had raised a man from the dead appear to his opponents so dangerous that they asked the question, "Can Jesus and Judaism exist side by side?" It does not do to assert with Renan: "The other miracles of Jesus were passing events, repeated in good faith and exaggerated by popular report, and they were thought no more of after they had happened. But this one was a real event, publicly known, and by means of which it was sought to silence the Pharisees. All the enemies of Jesus were exasperated by the sensation it caused. It is related that they sought to kill Lazarus." It is incomprehensible why this should be if

Renan were right in his opinion that all that happened at Bethany was the getting up of a mock scene, intended to strengthen belief in Jesus. "Perhaps Lazarus, still pale from his illness, had himself wrapped in a shroud and laid in the family grave. These tombs were large rooms hewn out of the rock, and entered by a square opening which was closed by an immense slab. Martha and Mary hastened to meet Jesus, and brought him to the grave before he had entered Bethany. The painful emotion felt by Jesus at the grave of the friend whom he believed to be dead (John xi. 33, 38) might be taken by those present for the agitation and tremors which were wont to accompany miracles. According to popular belief, divine power in a man was like an epileptic and convulsive element. Continuing the above hypothesis, Jesus wished to see once more the man he had loved, and the stone having been rolled away, Lazarus came forth in his grave-clothes, his head bound with a napkin. This apparition naturally was looked upon by every one as a resurrection. Faith knows no other law than the interest of what it holds to be true." Does not such an explanation appear absolutely naïve, when Renan adds the following opinion: "Everything seems to suggest that the miracle of Bethany materially contributed to hasten the death of Jesus"? Yet there is undoubtedly an accurate perception underlying this last assertion of Renan. But with the means at his disposal he is not able to interpret or justify his opinion.

Something of quite special importance must have been accomplished by Jesus at Bethany, in order that such words as the following may be accounted for: "Then gathered the chief priests and the Pharisees a council, and said, 'What do we? for this man doeth many miracles'" (John xi. 47). Renan, too, conjectures something special: "It must be acknowledged," he says, "that John's narrative is of an essentially different kind from the accounts of miracles of which the Synoptists are full, and which are the outcome of the popular imagination. Let us add that John is the only Evangelist with accurate knowledge of the relations of Jesus with the family at Bethany, and that it would be incomprehensible how a creation of the popular mind could have been inserted in the frame of such personal reminiscences. It is, therefore, probable that the miracle in question was not amongst the wholly legendary ones, for which no one is responsible. In other words, I think that something took place at Bethany which was looked upon as a resurrection." Does not this really mean that Renan surmises that something happened at Bethany which he cannot explain? He entrenches himself behind the words: "At this distance of time, and with only one text bearing obvious traces of subsequent additions, it is impossible to decide whether, in the present case, all is fiction, or whether a real fact which happened at Bethany served as the basis of the report that was spread abroad." Might it not be that we have to do here with something of which we might arrive at a true understanding merely by reading the text in the right way? In that case, we should perhaps no longer speak of "fiction."

It must be admitted that the whole narrative of this event in St. John's Gospel is wrapped in a mysterious veil. To show this, we need only mention one point. If the narrative is to be taken in the literal, physical sense, what meaning have these words of Jesus: "This sickness is not unto death, but for the glory of God, that the Son of God might be glorified thereby." This is the usual translation of the words, but the actual state of the case is better arrived at, if they are translated, "for the vision (or manifestation) of God, that the Son of God might be manifested thereby." This translation is also correct according to the Greek original. And what do these other words mean, "Jesus said unto her, I am the resurrection, and the life: he that believeth in me, though he were dead, yet shall he live"? (John xi. 4, 25). It would be a triviality to think that Jesus meant to say that Lazarus had only become ill in order that Jesus might manifest His skill through him. And it would again be a triviality to think that Jesus meant to assert that faith in Him brings to life again one who in the ordinary sense is dead. What would there be remarkable about a person who has risen from the dead, if after his resurrection he were the same as he was before dying? Indeed what would be the meaning of describing the life of such a person in the words, "I am the resurrection and the life"? Life and meaning at once come into the words of Jesus if we understand them to be the expression of a spiritual occurrence and then, in a certain sense, literally as they stand in the text. Jesus actually says that He is the resurrection that has happened to Lazarus, and that He is the life that Lazarus is living. Let us take literally what Jesus is in St. John's Gospel.

He is "the Word that was made flesh." He is the Eternal that existed in the beginning. If he is really the resurrection, then the Eternal, Primordial has risen again in Lazarus. We have, therefore, to do with a resurrection of the eternal "Word," and this "Word" is the life to which Lazarus has been raised. It is a case of illness, not one leading to death, but to the glory, *i.e.*, the manifestation of God. If the eternal Word has reawakened in Lazarus, the whole event conduces to manifest God in Lazarus. For by means of the event Lazarus has become a different man. Before it, the Word, or spirit did not live in him, now it does. The spirit has been born within him. It is true that every birth is accompanied by illness, that of the mother, but the illness leads to new life, not to death. In Lazarus that part of him becomes ill from which the "new man," permeated by the "Word," is born.

Where is the grave from which the "Word" is born? To answer this question we have only to remember Plato, who calls man's body the tomb of the soul.

And we have only to recall Plato's speaking of a kind of resurrection when he alludes to the coming to life of the spiritual world in the body. What Plato calls the spiritual soul, St. John denominates the "Word." And for him, Christ is the "Word." Plato might have said, "One who becomes spiritual has caused something divine to rise out of the grave of his body." For St. John, that which took place through the life of Jesus was that resurrection. It is not surprising, therefore, if he makes Jesus say, "I am the resurrection."

There can be no doubt that the occurrence at Bethany was an awakening in the spiritual sense. Lazarus became something different from what he was before. He was raised to a life of which the Eternal Word could say, "I am that life." What then took place in Lazarus? The spirit came to life within him. He became a partaker of the life which is eternal. We have only to express his experience in the words of those who were initiated into the Mysteries, and the meaning at once becomes clear. What does Plutarch (*vide supra* p. 26 *et seq.*) say about the object of the Mysteries? They were to serve to withdraw the soul from bodily life and to unite it with the gods. Schelling thus describes the feelings of an initiate:

"The initiate through his initiation became a link in the magic chain, he himself became a Kabir. He was admitted into an indestructible association and, as ancient inscriptions express it, joined to the army of the higher gods" (Schelling, *Philosophie der Offenbarung*). And the revolution that took place in the life of one who received initiation cannot be more significantly described than in the words spoken by Ädesius to his disciple, the Emperor Constantine: "If one day thou shouldst take part in the Mysteries, thou wilt feel ashamed of having been born merely as a man."

If we fill our souls with such feelings as these, we shall gain the right attitude towards the event that took place at Bethany, and have a peculiarly characteristic experience through St. John's narrative. A certainty will dawn upon us which cannot be obtained by any logical interpretation or by any attempt at rationalistic explanation. A mystery in the true sense of the word is before us. The "Eternal Word" entered into Lazarus. In the language of the Mysteries, he became an initiate (*vide* p. 132 *et seq.*), and the event narrated to us must be the process of initiation.

Let us look upon the whole occurrence as though it were an initiation. Lazarus is loved by Jesus (John xi. 36). No ordinary affection can be meant by this, for it would be contrary to the spirit of St. John's Gospel, in which Jesus is "The Word." Jesus loved Lazarus because he found him ripe for the awakening of "the Word" within him. Jesus had relations with the family at Bethany. This only means that Jesus had made everything ready in that family for the final act of the drama, the raising of Lazarus. The latter was a disciple of Jesus, such an one that Jesus could be quite sure that in him the awakening would be consummated. The final act in a drama of awakening consisted in a symbolical action. The person involved in it had not only to understand the words, "Die and become!" He had to fulfil them himself by a real, spiritual action. His earthly part, of which his higher being in the Spirit of the Mysteries must be ashamed, had to be put away. The earthly must die a symbolic-real death. The putting of his body into a somnambulic sleep for three days can only be denoted an outer event in comparison with the greatness of the transformation which was taking place in him. An incomparably more momentous spiritual event corresponded to it. But this very process was the experience which divides the life of the Mystic into two parts. One who does not know from experience the inner significance of such acts cannot understand them. They can only be suggested by means of a comparison.

The substance of Shakespeare's *Hamlet* may be compressed into a few words. Any one who learns these words may say that in a certain sense he knows the contents of *Hamlet*; and logically he does. But one who has let all the wealth of the Shakespearian drama stream in upon him knows *Hamlet* in a different way. A life-current has passed through his soul which cannot be replaced by any mere description. The idea of *Hamlet* has become an artistic, personal experience within him.

On a higher plane of consciousness, a similar process takes place in man when he experiences the magically significant event which is bound up with initiation. What he attains spiritually, he lives through symbolically. The word "symbolically" is used here in the sense that an outer event is really enacted on the physical plane, but that as such, it is nevertheless a symbol. It is not a case of an unreal, but of a real symbol. The earthly body has really been dead for three days.[5] New life comes forth from death. This life has outlived death. Man has gained confidence in the new life.

It happened thus with Lazarus. Jesus had prepared him for resurrection. His illness was at once symbolic and real, an illness which was an initiation (*cf.* p. 132 *et seq.*), and which leads, after three days, to a really new life.

Lazarus was ripe for undergoing this experience. He wrapped himself in the garment of the Mystic, and fell into a condition of lifelessness which was symbolic death. And when Jesus came, the three days had elapsed. "Then they took away the stone from the place where the dead was laid. And Jesus lifted up his eyes and said, 'Father, I thank thee that thou hast heard me'" (John xi. 41). The Father had heard Jesus, for Lazarus had come to the final act in the great drama of knowledge. He had learned how resurrection is attained. An initiation into the Mysteries had been consummated. It was a case of such an initiation as had been understood as such during the whole of antiquity. It had taken place through Jesus, as the initiator. Union with the divine had always been conceived of in this way.

In Lazarus Jesus accomplished the great miracle of the transmutation of life in the sense of immemorial tradition. Through this event, Christianity is connected with the Mysteries. Lazarus had become an initiate through Christ Jesus Himself, and had thereby become able to enter the higher worlds. He was at once the first Christian initiate and the first to be initiated by Christ Jesus Himself. Through his initiation he had become capable of recognising that the "Word" which had been awakened within him had become a person in Christ Jesus, and that consequently there stood before him in the personality of his awakener, the same force which had been spiritually manifested within him. From this point of view, these words of Jesus are significant, "And I knew that thou hearest me always: but because of the people which stand by I said it, that they may believe that thou hast sent me." This means that the point is to make evident this fact: in Jesus lives the "Son of the Father" in such a way that when he awakens his own nature in man, man becomes a Mystic. In this way Jesus made it plain that the meaning of life was hidden in the Mysteries and that they were the path to this understanding. He is the living Word; in Him was personified what had been immemorial tradition. And therefore the Evangelist is justified in expressing this in the sentence, "in Him the Word was made flesh." He rightly sees in Jesus himself an incarnated Mystery. On this account, St. John's Gospel is a Mystery. In order to read it rightly, we must bear in mind that the facts are spiritual facts. If a priest of the old order had written it, he would have described traditional rites. These for St. John took the form of a person, and became the life of Jesus.

An eminent modern investigator of the Mysteries, Burkhardt in *Die Zeit Konstantins*, says that they "will never be cleared up." This is because he has not found out how to explain them. If we take the Gospel of St. John and see in it the working out in symbolic-corporeal reality the drama of knowledge presented by the ancients, we are really gazing upon the Mystery itself.

In the words, "Lazarus, come forth," we can recognise the call with which the Egyptian priestly initiators summoned back to every-day life those who, temporarily removed from the world by the processes of initiation, had undergone them in order to die to earthly things and to gain a conviction of the reality of the eternal. Jesus in this way revealed the secret of the Mysteries. It is easy to understand that the Jews could not let such an act go unpunished, any more than the Greeks could have refrained from punishing Æschylus, if he had betrayed the secrets of the Mysteries.

The main point for Jesus was to represent in the initiation of Lazarus before all "the people which stood by," an event which in the old days of priestly wisdom could only be enacted in the recesses of the mystery-temples. The initiation of Lazarus was to prepare the way to the understanding of the "Mystery of Golgotha." Previously only those who "saw," that is to say, who were initiated, were able to know something of what was achieved by initiation, but now a conviction of the Mysteries of higher worlds could also be gained by those who "had not seen, and yet had believed."

FOOTNOTES:

[5] This and other circumstances connected with the so-called raising of Lazarus from the dead are to be understood in the light of the fact, that Lazarus' death-sleep was at the same time symbolic and real—it was in other words a symbolic reality, a reality symbolising other realities, and but for the action of Christ, Lazarus would have remained dead.

IX

THE APOCALYPSE OF ST. JOHN

At the end of the New Testament stands a remarkable document, the Apocalypse, the secret Revelation of St. John. We have only to read the opening words to feel the deep mystic character of this book. "The Revelation of Jesus Christ, which God gave unto him, to shew unto his servants how the necessary things are shortly going to happen; and this is sent in signs by the angel of God unto his servant John." What is here revealed is "sent in signs." Therefore we must not take the literal meaning of the words as they stand, but seek for a deeper meaning of which the words are only signs. But there are other things also which point to a hidden meaning. St. John addresses himself to the seven churches in Asia. Not actual, material churches are meant; the number seven is the sacred number, chosen on account of its symbolic meaning. The actual number of the Asiatic churches was different. And the manner in which St. John arrived at the revelation also points to something mysterious. "I was in the Spirit on the Lord's day, and heard behind me a great voice, as of a trumpet, saying, 'What thou seest, write in a book, and send it unto the seven churches.'" Thus, we have to do with a revelation received by St. John in the spirit. And it is the revelation of Jesus Christ. Wrapped in a hidden meaning there appears what Christ Jesus manifested to the world. Therefore we must also look for this hidden meaning in the teachings of Christ. This revelation bears the same relation to ordinary Christianity as was borne by the revelation of the Mysteries, in pre-Christian times, to the people's religion. On this account the attempt to treat the Apocalypse as a mystery appears to be justified.

The Apocalypse is addressed to seven churches. For the reason of this we have only to single out one of the seven messages sent. In the first of these it is said, "Unto the angel of the church of Ephesus write; these things saith he that holdeth the seven stars in his right hand, who walketh in the midst of the seven golden candlesticks; I know thy works, and thy labour, and thy patience, and how thou canst not bear them which are evil: and thou hast tried them which say they are apostles, and are not, and hast found them liars: and hast borne, and hast patience, and for my name's sake hast laboured, and hast not fainted. Nevertheless I have somewhat against thee, because thou hast left thy highest love. Remember therefore from whence thou art fallen, and repent, and do the best works; or else I will come unto thee quickly, and will remove thy candlestick out of his place, except thou repent. But this thou hast, that thou hatest the deeds of the Nicolaitanes, which I also hate. He that hath an ear, let him hear what the Spirit saith unto the churches; to him that overcometh will I give to eat of the tree of life, which is in the midst of the paradise of God." This is the message addressed to the angel of the first community. The angel, who represents the spirit of this community, has entered upon the path pointed out by Christianity. He is able to distinguish between the false adherents of Christianity and the true. He wishes to be Christian, and has founded his work on the name of Christ. But it is required of him that he should not bar his own way to the highest love by any kind of mistakes. He is shown the possibility of taking a wrong course through such errors. Through Christ Jesus the way for attaining to the divine has been pointed out. Perseverance is needed for advancing further in the spirit in which the first impulse was given. It is possible to believe too soon that one has the right spirit. This happens when the disciple lets himself be led a short way by Christ and then leaves his leadership, giving way to false ideas about it. The disciple thereby falls back again into the lower self. He has left his "highest love." The knowledge which is attached to the senses and intellect may be raised into a higher sphere, becoming wisdom, by being spiritualised and made divine. If it does not reach this height, it remains amongst perishable things. Christ Jesus has pointed out the path to the Eternal, and knowledge must with unwearied perseverance follow the path which leads to its becoming divine. Lovingly must it trace out the methods which transmute it into wisdom. The Nicolaitanes were a sect who took Christianity too lightly. They saw one thing only, that Christ is the Divine Word, the Eternal Wisdom which is born in man. Therefore they concluded that human wisdom was the Divine Word, and that it was enough to pursue human knowledge in order to realise the divine in the world. But the meaning of Christian wisdom cannot be construed thus. The knowledge which in the first instance is human wisdom is as perishable as anything else, unless it is first transmuted into divine wisdom. "Thou art not thus," says the "Spirit" to the angel of Ephesus; "thou hast 'not relied' merely upon human wisdom. Thou hast patiently trodden the Christian path. But thou must not think that the 'highest' love is not needed to attain to the goal. Such a love is necessary which far surpasses all love to other things. Only such can be the 'highest' love. The path to the divine is an infinite one, and it is to be understood that when the first step has been gained, it can only be the preparation for ascending higher and higher." Such is the first of these messages, as they are to be interpreted. The meaning of the others may be found in a similar way.

St. John turned, and saw "seven golden candlesticks," and "in the midst of the seven candlesticks one like unto the Son of Man, clothed with a garment down to the foot, and girt about the paps with a golden girdle. His head and his hairs were white like wool, as white as snow; and his eyes were as a flame of fire." We are told (i. 20) that "the seven candlesticks are the seven churches." This means that the candlesticks are seven different ways of attaining to the divine. They are all more or less imperfect. And the Son of Man "had in his right hand seven stars" (v. 16). The seven stars are the angels of the seven churches (v. 20). The guiding spirits, or daimons (*cf.* p. 87), of the wisdom of the Mysteries have here become the guiding angels of the churches. The churches are represented as bodies for spiritual beings, and the angels are the souls of those bodies, just as human souls are the guiding powers of human bodies. The churches are the imperfect ways to the divine, and the souls of the churches were to become guides along those paths. For this purpose they must themselves have for their leader the being who has in his right hand seven stars. "And out of his mouth went a sharp two-edged sword: and his countenance was as the sun shineth in his strength." This sword is also found in the Mysteries. The candidate for initiation was terrified by a flashing sword (*cf.* p. 18). This indicates the situation of one who wishes to know the divine by experience, so that the face of wisdom may shine upon him like the sun. St. John also goes through this experience. It is to be a test of his strength (*cf.* p. 18). "And when I saw him, I fell at his feet as dead. And he laid his right hand upon me, saying unto me, Fear not" (v. 17). The candidate for initiation must pass through the experiences which otherwise man only undergoes at the gate of death. His guide must lead him beyond the region in which birth and death have a meaning. The initiate enters upon a new life. "And I was dead; and, behold, I am alive for evermore, Amen; and have the keys of hell and of death."

Thus prepared, St. John is led on to learn the secrets of existence. "After this I looked, and, behold, a door was opened in heaven: and the first voice which I heard was as it were of a trumpet talking with me; which said, Come up hither, and I will shew thee things which must be hereafter." The messages to the seven spirits of the churches make known to St. John what is to take place in the physical world in order to prepare the way for Christianity. What he now sees "in the Spirit" takes him to the spiritual fountain-head of things, hidden behind physical evolution, but which will be realised, in a spiritualised age, in the near future, by means of physical evolution. The initiate experiences now in the spirit what is to happen in the future,—"And immediately I was in the spirit: and, behold, a throne was set in heaven, and one sat on the throne. And he that sat was to look upon like a jasper and a sardine stone: and there was a rainbow round about the throne, in sight like unto an emerald." In this way is described the source of things in the world of sense, in the pictures in which it appears to the seer. "And round about the throne were four and twenty seats: and upon the seats I saw four and twenty elders sitting, clothed in white raiment; and they had on their heads crowns of gold" (iv. 2-4). The beings far advanced on the path of wisdom thus surround the fountain-head of existence, to gaze on its infinite essence and bear testimony to it. "And in the midst of the throne, and round about the throne, were four beasts full of eyes before and behind. And the first beast was like a lion, and the second beast like a calf, and the third beast had a face as a man, and the fourth beast was like a flying eagle. And the four beasts had each of them six wings about him; and they were full of eyes within: and they rest not day and night, saying, Holy, holy, holy, Lord God Almighty, which was, and is, and is to come." It is not difficult to see that the four beasts represent the supersensible life underlying physical forms of life. Afterwards, when the trumpets sound, they lift up their voices, *i.e.*, when the life expressed in sense-forms has been transmuted into spiritual life.

In the right hand of him who sits on the throne is the book in which the path to the highest wisdom is traced out (v. 1). There is only one worthy to open the book. "Behold, the Lion of the tribe of Juda, the Root of David, hath prevailed to open the book and to loose the seven seals thereof." The seven seals of the book denote that human wisdom is sevenfold. That this is so is again connected with the sacred character of the number seven. The mystic wisdom of Philo designates as seals the eternal cosmic thoughts which come to expression in things. Human wisdom seeks for those creative thoughts; but only in the book, which is sealed with them, is divine truth to be found. The fundamental thoughts of creation must first be unveiled, the seals must be opened, before what is in the book can be revealed. Jesus, the Lion, has power to open the seals. He has given a direction to the great creative thoughts which, through them, leads to wisdom. The Lamb that was slain and that has bought its divinity with its blood, Jesus, who drew down the Christ into Himself and who thus, in the supreme sense, passed through the Life-Death-Mystery, opens the book (v. 9, 10). And as each seal is opened (vi), the four beasts declare what they know.

At the opening of the first seal, St. John sees a white horse, on which sits a rider with a bow. The first universal power, an embodiment of Creative Thought, becomes visible. It is put into the right direction by the new rider, Christianity. Strife is allayed by the new faith. At the opening of the second seal a red horse appears, ridden by one who takes away from the earth Peace,—the second universal power, so that humanity may not neglect, through sloth, to cultivate divine things. The opening of the third seal shows the universal power of Justice, guided by Christianity. The fourth brings the power of Religion which, through Christianity, has received new dignity.

The meaning of the four beasts thus becomes plain. They are the four chief universal powers, to which Christianity gives a new direction: War (the lion); Peaceful Work (the bull); Justice (the being with the human face); and Religious Enthusiasm (the eagle). The meaning of the third being becomes clear when it is said, at the opening of the third seal, "A measure of wheat for a penny, and three measures of barley for a penny," and that the rider holds "a pair of balances." And at the opening of the fourth seal a rider becomes visible whose name "was Death, and Hell followed with him." This rider is Religious Justice (vi. 6, 8). When the fifth seal is opened there appear the souls of those who have already acted in the spirit of Christianity. Creative thought itself, embodied in Christianity, shows itself here; but by this Christianity is at first meant only the first Christian community, which was transitory like other forms of creation. The sixth seal is opened (vi.); it is made evident that the spiritual world of Christianity is an eternal world. The people at large seem to be permeated by that spiritual world out of which Christianity itself proceeded. What it has itself created becomes sanctified. "And I heard the number of them which were sealed: and there were sealed an hundred and forty and four thousand of all the tribes of the children of Israel" (vii. 4). They are those who prepared for the Eternal before the coming of Christianity, and who were transformed by the Christ-impulse.

The opening of the seventh seal follows. It becomes evident what true Christianity is to be in the evolution of the world. The seven angels, "which stood before God," appear (Rev. viii. 2). Again these angels are spirits from the ancient Mysteries transferred to Christianity. They are the spirits who lead to the vision of God in a really Christian way. Therefore what is next accomplished is a leading to God: it is an "initiation" which is bestowed upon St. John. The proclamations of the angels are accompanied by the necessary signs during initiations. "The first angel sounded and there followed hail and fire mingled with blood, and they were cast upon the earth: and the third part of trees was burnt up, and all green grass was burnt up." And similar things take place when the other angels sound their trumpets.

At this point we see that this was not merely an initiation in the old sense, but that a new one was taking the place of the old. Christianity was not to be confined, like the ancient Mysteries, to a few elect ones. It was to belong to the whole of humanity. It was to be a religion of the people; the truth was to be ready for each one who "has ears to hear." The old Mystics were singled out from a great number; the trumpets of Christianity sound for every one who is willing to hear them. Whether he draws near or not depends on himself. This is the reason why the terrors accompanying this initiation of humanity are so enormously enhanced. What is to become of the earth and its inhabitants in a far distant future is revealed to St. John at his initiation. Underlying this is the thought that initiates are able to foresee in higher worlds what is realised in the lower world only in the future. The seven messages present the meaning of Christianity to that age, the seven seals represent what was then being prepared through Christianity for future accomplishment. The future is veiled and sealed to the uninitiated; it is unsealed in initiation. When the earthly period is over during which the seven messages hold good, a more spiritual time will begin. Then life will no more flow on as it appears in physical forms, but even outwardly it will be a copy of its supersensible forms. These latter are represented by the four animals and the other seal-pictures. In a still later future appears that form of the earth which the initiate experiences through the trumpets.

Thus the initiate prophetically goes through what is to happen. And the Christian initiate learns how the Christ-impulse interposes and works on in earthly evolution. After it has been shown how all that is too much attached to perishable things perishes to attain true Christianity, there appears the mighty angel with a little book open in his hand, which he gives to St. John. "And he said unto me, Take it, and eat it up; and it shall make thy belly bitter, but it shall be in thy mouth sweet as honey" (x. 9). St. John was not only to read the little book, he was to absorb it and let its contents permeate him. What avails any knowledge unless man is vitally and thoroughly imbued with it? Wisdom has to become life, man must not merely recognise the divine, but become divine himself. Such wisdom as is written in the book no doubt causes pain to the perishable part of man, "it shall make thy belly bitter," but so much the more does it make happy the eternal part, "but it shall be in thy mouth sweet as honey."

Only by such an initiation can Christianity become actual on the earth. It kills everything belonging to the lower nature. "And their dead bodies shall lie in the street of the great city, which spiritually is called Sodom and Egypt, where also our Lord was crucified." By this is meant the followers of Christ, who are ill-treated by the temporal powers. But what is ill-treated is only the mortal part of human nature, which they will afterwards have conquered. Thereby their fate is a copy of the prefiguring fate of Christ Jesus. "Spiritually Sodom and Egypt" is the symbol of a life which cleaves to the outer and is not changed by the Christ-impulse. Christ is everywhere crucified in the lower nature. When the lower nature conquers, all remains dead. The dead bodies of men lie about in the public places of cities. Those who overcome the lower nature and awaken the crucified Christ hear the trumpet of the seventh angel, "the kingdoms of this world are become the kingdoms of our Lord, and of his Christ, and he shall reign for ever and ever" (xi. 15). "And the temple of God was opened in heaven, and there was seen in his temple the ark of his testament" (xi. 19).

In the vision of these events, the initiate sees renewed the old struggle between the lower and the higher natures. For everything which the candidate for initiation formerly had to go through must be repeated in one who follows the Christian path. Just as Osiris was threatened by the evil Typhon so now "the great dragon, that old serpent" (xii. 9) must be overcome. The woman, the human soul, gives birth to lower knowledge, which is an adverse power if it is not raised to wisdom. Man must pass through that lower knowledge. In the Apocalypse it appears as the "old serpent." From the remotest times the serpent had been the symbol of knowledge in all mystic wisdom. Man may be led astray by this serpent,—

knowledge,—if he does not bring to life in him the Son of God, who crushes the serpent's head. "And the great dragon was cast out, that old serpent, called the Devil, and Satan, which deceiveth the whole world: he was cast out into the earth, and his angels were cast out with him" (xii. 9). In these words we can see what it was that Christianity wished to be:—a new kind of initiation. What had been attained in the Mysteries was to be attained in a new form. For in them too the serpent had to be overcome, but this was no longer to take place in the old way. The one, primeval mystery, the Christian mystery, was to replace the many mysteries of antiquity. Jesus, in whom the Logos had been made flesh, was to become the initiator of the whole of humanity, and humanity was to be his own community of Mystics.

What was to take place was not a separation of the elect, but a linking together of all. As each grows up to it so does he become a Mystic. The good tidings are announced to all, he who has an ear to hear hastens to learn the secrets. The voice of the heart is to decide in each individual case. It is not that one person at a time is introduced into the Mystery-temples, but that the word is to be spoken to all, to one it will then appeal more strongly than to another. It will be left to the daimon, the angel within each individual, to decide how far the latter may be initiated. The whole world is a Mystery-temple. Not only is salvation to come to those who see the wonderful processes in the special temples for initiation,—processes which give them a guarantee of eternal life, but "Blessed are they that have not seen, and yet have believed." Even if at first they grope in the dark, the light may nevertheless come to them later. Nothing is to be withheld from any one; the way is to be open to all.

The latter part of the Apocalypse describes clearly the dangers threatening Christianity through anti-Christian powers, and the final triumph of Christianity. All other gods are merged in the one Christian divinity: "And the city had no need of the sun, neither of the moon to shine in it: for the glory of God did lighten it, and the Lamb is the light thereof" (xxi. 23). The secret of the Revelation of St. John is that the Mysteries are no longer to be kept under lock and key. "And he saith unto me, Seal not the sayings of the prophecy of this book, for the time is at hand."

The author of the Apocalypse has set forth what he believes to be the relation of his church to the churches of antiquity. He wished to express in a spiritual mystery what he thought about the Mysteries themselves. He wrote his mystery on the isle of Patmos, and he is said to have received the "Revelation" in a grotto. These details indicate that the revelation was of a mystery character.

Thus Christianity arose out of the Mysteries. Its wisdom is born as a mystery in the Apocalypse, but a mystery which transcends the limits of the old mystery world. The separate Mysteries were to become one universal one.

It may appear to be a contradiction to say that the secrets of the Mysteries became manifest through Christianity, and that nevertheless a Christian mystery is to be seen again in the spiritual visions of the writer of the Apocalypse. The contradiction disappears directly we reflect that the secrets of the ancient Mysteries were revealed by the events in Palestine. Through these there became manifest what had previously been veiled in the Mysteries. There is now a new secret, namely what has been introduced into the evolution of the world by the appearance of the Christ. The initiate of ancient times, when in the spiritual world, saw how evolution points the way to the as yet hidden Christ. The Christian initiate experiences the unseen effects of the manifested Christ.

X

JESUS AND HIS HISTORICAL BACKGROUND

In the wisdom of the Mysteries is to be sought the soil out of which grew the spirit of Christianity. All that was needed was the gaining ground of the fundamental conviction that this spirit must be introduced into life in greater measure than had been the case with the Mysteries. But such a conviction was widely spread, as may be seen from the manner of life of the Essenes and Therapeutæ, who existed long before Christianity arose.

The Essenes were a secluded sect, living in Palestine, whose numbers at the time of Christ were estimated at four thousand. They formed a community which required that its members should lead a life which developed a higher life within the soul, and brought about a new birth. The aspirant for admission was subjected to a severe test, in order to ascertain whether he were ripe for preparing himself for a higher life. If he was admitted, he had to undergo a period of probation, and to take a solemn oath that he would not betray to strangers the secrets of the Essenian discipline. The object of this life was the conquest of the lower nature in man, so that the spirit latent within him might be awakened ever more and more. One who had experienced up to a certain point the spirit within him was raised to a higher grade, and enjoyed a corresponding degree of authority, not forced from without, but conditioned by the nature of things.

Akin to the Essenes were the Therapeutæ, who dwelt in Egypt. We get all desirable details of their mode of life in a treatise by the philosopher Philo, *On the Contemplative Life*. (The dispute as to the authenticity of this work must now be regarded as settled, and it may be rightly assumed that Philo really described the life of a community existing long before Christianity, and well known to him. *Cf.* on the subject, G.R. Mead's *Fragments of a Faith Forgotten*.) A few passages from Philo's treatise will give an idea of the main tenets of the Therapeutæ. "The dwellings of the members of the community are extremely simple, only affording necessary shelter from extreme heat and cold. The dwellings are not built close together, as in towns, for contiguity has no attraction for one who wishes for solitude; nor are they at a great distance one from another, in order that the social relations, so dear to them, may not be made difficult, and that they may easily be able to assist each other in case of an attack by brigands. In each house is a consecrated room called a temple or monasterion, a small room or cell in which the mysteries of the higher life are cultivated.... They also possess works by ancient authors who once directed their school, and left behind many explanations about the customary method used in allegorical writings.... Their interpretation of sacred writings is directed to the deeper meaning of allegorical narratives."

We thus see that what had been striven after in the narrower circle of the Mysteries was being made general. But such a generalisation naturally weakened their severe character. The Essene and Therapeutic communities form a natural transition from the Mysteries to Christianity. But Christianity wished to extend to humanity in general what with the Essenes and Therapeutæ was an affair of a sect. This of course prepared the way for a still further weakening of the old severe forms.

The existence of such sects makes it possible to understand how far the time was ripe for the comprehension of the mystery of Christ. In the Mysteries, a man was artificially prepared for the dawning upon his consciousness, at the appropriate time, of the spiritual world. Within the Essene or Therapeutic community the soul sought, by a certain mode of life, to become ripe for the awakening of the higher man. A further step forward is that man struggles through to a feeling that a human individuality may have evolved to higher and higher stages of perfection in repeated earth lives. One who had arrived at a glimpse of this truth would also be able to feel that in Jesus a being of lofty spirituality had appeared. The loftier the spirituality, the greater the possibility of accomplishing something of importance. Thus the individuality of Jesus could become capable of accomplishing the deed which the Evangelists so mysteriously indicate in the Baptism by John, and which, by the way in which they speak of it, they so clearly point out as of the utmost importance. The personality of Jesus became able to receive into its own soul Christ, the Logos, who was made flesh in that soul. Thenceforward the Ego of Jesus of Nazareth was the Christ, and the outer personality was the vehicle of the Logos. The event of the Ego of Jesus becoming the Christ is enacted in the Baptism by St. John. During the period of the Mysteries, "union with the Spirit" was only for those who were initiated. Amongst the Essenes, a whole community cultivated a life by means of which all its members were able to arrive at the mystical union. In the coming of Christ, something, *i.e.*, the deeds of Christ, was placed before the whole of humanity, so that all might share in the mystical union.

XI

THE NATURE OF CHRISTIANITY

The deepest effect must have been produced upon believers in Christianity by the fact that the Divine, the Word, the eternal Logos, no longer came to them in the dim twilight of the Mysteries, as Spirit only, but that when they spoke of the Logos, they were made to think of the historical, human personality of Jesus. Formerly the Logos had only been seen in different degrees of human perfection. The delicate, subtle differences in the spiritual life of personalities could be observed, and the manner and degree in which the Logos became living within those seeking initiation. A higher degree of maturity was to be interpreted as a higher stage of evolution of spiritual life. The preparatory steps had to be sought in a spiritual life already passed through, and the present life was to be regarded as the preparatory stage for future degrees of spiritual evolution. The conservation of the spiritual power of the soul and the eternity of that force might be stated in the words of the Jewish occult teaching in the book of Sohar, "Nothing in the world is lost, nothing falls into the void, not even the words and voice of man: everything has its place and purport." Personality was but a metamorphosis of the soul, which develops from one personality to another. The single life of the personality was only considered as a link in the chain of development stretching backwards and forwards.

This Logos metamorphosing itself in the many separate human personalities has through Christianity been directed away from these to the one unique personality of Jesus. What had previously been distributed throughout the world was now united in a single personality. Jesus became the unique God-Man. In Jesus something was present once which must appear to man as the greatest of ideals, and with which, in the course of man's repeated earthly lives, he ought to be more and more united. Jesus took upon Himself the divinisation of the whole of humanity. In Him was sought what formerly could only be sought in a man's own particular soul. One did not any more behold the divine and eternal within the personality of a man; all that was now beheld in Jesus. It is not the eternal part of the soul that conquers death and is raised through its own power as divine, but it is that which was in Jesus, the one God that will appear and raise the souls.

It follows from this that an entirely new meaning was given to personality. The eternal, immortal part had been taken from it. Only the personality, as such, was left. If immortality be not denied, it has to be admitted as pertaining to the personality itself. Out of the belief in the soul's eternal metamorphosis came the belief in personal immortality. The personality acquired infinite importance, because it was the only thing which was left to man.

Henceforth there is nothing between the personality and the infinite God. A direct relation with Him must be established. Man was no longer capable of himself becoming divine, in a greater or less degree. He was simply man, standing in a direct but outward relation to God. This brought quite a new note into the conception of the world for those who knew the point of view held in the ancient Mysteries. There were many people in this position during the first centuries of Christianity. They knew the nature of the Mysteries. If they wished to become Christians, they were obliged to come to an understanding with the older conceptions. This brought them most difficult conflicts within their souls. They sought in most various ways to effect a settlement between the two tendencies in the conception of the world. This conflict is reflected in the writings of early Christian times: in those of heathens attracted by the sublimity of Christianity, as well as in the writings of those Christians who found it hard to give up the conceptions of the Mysteries. Slowly did Christianity grow out of these Mysteries. On the one hand Christian convictions were presented in the form of the Mystery truths, and on the other, the Mystery wisdom was clothed in Christian words.

Clement of Alexandria (ob. 217 A.D.), a Christian writer whose education had been pagan, is an instance of this, "God has not forbidden us to rest from good deeds when keeping the sabbath. He permits those who can grasp them to share in the divine mysteries and in the sacred light. He has not revealed to the crowd what is not suitable for them. He judged it fitting to reveal it only to a few, who are able to grasp it and to work out in themselves the unspeakable mystery which God confided to the Logos, not to the written word. And God hath set some in the Church as apostles; and some prophets; and some evangelists; and some pastors and teachers; for the perfecting of the saints, for the work of the ministry, for the edifying of the body of Christ." Individual souls in those days sought by very different paths to find the way from the ancient views to the Christian ones. And the one who thought he was on the right path called others heretics. In the meanwhile, the Church grew stronger and stronger as an outward institution. The more power it gained, the more did the path, recognised as the right one by the decisions of councils, take the place of personal investigation. It was for the Church to decide who deviated too far from the divine truth which she guarded. The idea of a "heretic" took firmer and firmer shape. During the first centuries of Christianity, the search for the divine path was a much more personal matter than it afterwards became. A long distance had been travelled before Augustine's conviction became possible: "I should not believe in the truth of the Gospels unless the authority of the Catholic Church forced me to do so" (*cf.* p. 143).

The conflict between the method of the Mysteries and that of the Christian religion acquired a special stamp through the various Gnostic sects and writers. We may class as Gnostics all the writers of the first Christian centuries who sought for a deep, spiritual meaning in Christian teachings. (A brilliant account of the development of the Gnosis is given in G.R.S. Mead's book mentioned above, *Fragments of a Faith Forgotten*.) We understand the Gnostics when we look upon them as saturated with the ancient wisdom of the Mysteries, and striving to understand Christianity from that point of view. For them, Christ was the Logos, and as such of a spiritual nature. In His primal essence, He cannot approach man from without. He must be awakened in the soul. But the historical Jesus must bear some relation to the spiritual Logos. This was the crucial point for the Gnostics. Some settled it in one way, some in another. The essential point common to them all was that to arrive at a true understanding of the Christ-idea, mere historical tradition was not enough, but that it must be sought either in the wisdom of the Mysteries, or in the Neo-Platonic philosophy which was derived from the same source. The Gnostics had confidence in human wisdom, and believed it capable of bringing forth a Christ by whom the historical Christ could be measured: in fact, through whom alone the latter could be understood and beheld in the right light.

Of special interest from this point of view is the doctrine given in the books of Dionysius the Areopagite. It is true that there is no mention of these writings till the sixth century; it matters little when and where they were written, the point is that they give an account of Christianity which is clothed in the language of the Neo-Platonic philosophy and presented in the form of a spiritual contemplation of the higher world. At all events this is a form of delineation which belongs to the first Christian centuries. In older times the truth was handed on in the form of oral tradition; the most important things were not entrusted to writing. The Christianity described in the writings of Dionysius is set forth in the mirror of the Neo-Platonic conception of the world. Sense-perception troubles man's spiritual vision. He must reach out beyond the senses. But all human ideas are primarily derived from observation by the senses. What man perceives with his senses, he calls existence; what he does not so perceive, he calls non-existence. Therefore if he wishes to open up an actual view of the Divine, he must rise above existence and non-existence, for these also, as he conceives them, have their origin in the sphere of the senses. In this sense God is neither existent nor non-existent; he is super-existent. Consequently he cannot be attained by means of ordinary cognition, which has to do with existing things. We have to be raised above ourselves, above our sense-observation, above our reasoning logic, if we are to find the way to spiritual vision. Thence we are able to get a glimpse into the perspectives of the Divine.

But this super-existent Divinity has brought forth the Logos, the basis of the universe, filled with wisdom. To him man's lower powers are able to attain. He is present in the cosmos as the spiritual Son of God, he is the Mediator between God and man. He may be present in man in various degrees. He may for instance be realised in an external institution, in which those diversely imbued with his spirit are grouped into a hierarchy. A "church" of this kind is the outer reality of the Logos, and the power which lives in it lived in a personal way in the Christ become flesh, in Jesus. Thus the Church is through Jesus united to God: Jesus is its meaning and crowning-point.

One thing was clear to all Gnosis, that one must come to an understanding about the personality of Jesus. Christ and Jesus must be brought into connection with one another. Divinity was taken away from human personality and must, in one way or another, be recovered. It must be possible to find it again in Jesus. The Mystic had to do with a degree of divinity within himself, and with his earthly personality. The Christian had to do with the latter, and also with a perfect God, far above all that is attainable by humanity. If we hold firmly to this point of view, a fundamental mystic attitude of the soul is only possible when the soul's spiritual eyes are opened; when, through finding higher spiritual possibilities within itself, the soul throws itself open to the light which issues from Christ in Jesus. The union of the soul with its highest powers is at the same time union with the historical Christ. For mysticism is an immediate consciousness and feeling of the divine within the soul. But a God far transcending everything human can never dwell in the soul in the real sense of the word. The Gnosis and all subsequent Christian mysticism represent the effort, in some way or other, to lay hold of that God, and to apprehend Him directly in the soul.

A conflict in this case was inevitable. It was really only possible for a man to find his own divine part, but this is both human and divine,—the divine at a certain stage of development. Yet the Christian God is a definite one, perfect in himself. It was possible for a person to find in himself the power to strive upwards to this God, but he could not say that what he experienced in his own soul, at any stage of development, was one with God. A great gulf was fixed between what it was possible to find in the soul, and what Christianity called divine. It is the gulf between science and faith, between knowledge and religious feeling.

This gulf does not exist for the Mystic in the old sense of the word. For he knows for a certainty that he can only comprehend the divine by degrees, and he also knows why this is so. It is clear to him that this gradual attainment is a real attainment of real divine life, and he finds it difficult to speak of a perfect, isolated divine principle. A Mystic of this kind does not seek a perfect God, but he wishes to experience the divine life. He seeks to be made divine, not to gain an external relation to the Godhead.

It is of the essence of Christianity that its mysticism in this sense starts with an assumption. The Christian Mystic seeks to behold divinity within him, but at the same time he looks up to the historical Christ as his physical eyes do to the sun. Just as the sun is the means by which physical eyes behold physical objects, so does the Christian Mystic intensify his inner nature that it may behold the divine, and the light which makes such vision possible for him is the fact of the appearance of Christ. It is He who enables man to attain his highest possibilities. It is in this way that the Christian Mystics of the Middle Ages differ from the Mystics of the ancient Mysteries (*cf.* my book, *Mystics of the Renaissance*).

XII

CHRISTIANITY AND HEATHEN WISDOM

At the time of the first beginnings of Christianity, there appear in heathen civilisation conceptions of the universe which seem to be a continuation of the Platonic philosophy, and which may also be taken as a deepening and spiritualisation of the wisdom of the Mysteries. The beginning of such conceptions is to be dated from Philo of Alexandria (B.C. 25-A.D. 50). From his point of view the processes which lead to the divine take place in the innermost part of the human soul. We might say that the temple in which Philo seeks initiation is wholly within him, and his higher experiences are the Mysteries. In his case processes of a purely spiritual nature replace the initiatory ceremonies of the sanctuary.

According to Philo, sense-observation and knowledge gained through the logical intellect do not lead to the divine. They have merely to do with what is perishable. But there is a way by which the soul may rise above these methods. It must come out of what it calls its ordinary self: from this it must withdraw. Then it enters a state of spiritual exaltation and illumination, in which it no longer knows, thinks, and judges in the ordinary sense of the words; for it has become merged, identified with the divine, which is experienced in its essence, and cannot be imparted in thought-concepts or abstract ideas. It is experienced, and one who goes through this experience knows that no one can impart it, for the only way of reaching it is to live it. The visible world is an image of this mystic reality which is experienced in the inmost recesses of the soul. The world has come forth from the invisible, inconceivable God. The harmony of the cosmos, which is steeped in wisdom, and to which sense-phenomena are subject, is a direct reflection of the Godhead, its spiritual image. It is divine spirit poured out into the world,—cosmic reason, the Logos, the offspring or Son of God. The Logos is the mediator between the world of sense and the unimaginable God. When man steeps himself in knowledge, he becomes united with the Logos, which is embodied in him. The person who has developed spirituality is the vehicle of the Logos. Above the Logos is God; beneath is the perishable world. It is man's vocation to form the link between the two. What he experiences in his inmost being, as spirit, is the universal Spirit. Such ideas are directly reminiscent of the Pythagorean manner of thinking (*cf.* p. 57 *et seq.*).

The centre of existence is sought in the inner life, but this life is conscious of its cosmic value. St. Augustine was thinking in virtually the same way as Philo, when he said: "We see all created things because they are; but they are, because God sees them." And he adds, concerning what and how we see:

"And because they are, we see them outwardly; because they are perfect, we see them inwardly."

Plato has the same fundamental idea (*cf.* p. 63 *et seq.*). Like Plato, Philo sees in the destiny of the human soul the closing act of the great cosmic drama, the awakening of the divinity that is under a spell. He thus describes the inner actions of the soul: the wisdom in man's inner being walks along, "tracing the paths of the Father, and shapes the forms while beholding the archetypes." It is no personal matter for man to create forms in his inner being; they are the eternal wisdom, they are the cosmic life.

This is in harmony with the interpretation of the myths of the people in the light of the Mysteries. The Mystic searches for the deeper truth in the myths (*cf.* p. 94 *et seq.*). And as the Mystic treats the myths of paganism, Philo handles Moses' story of the creation. The Old Testament accounts are for him images of inner soul-processes. The Bible relates the creation of the world. One who merely takes it as a description of outer events only half knows it. It is certainly written, "In the beginning God created the heaven and the earth. And the earth was without form and void, and darkness was on the face of the deep. And the spirit of God moved on the face of the waters." But the real inner meaning of the words must be lived in the depths of the soul. God must be found within, then He appears as the "Primal Splendour, who sends out innumerable rays, not perceptible by the senses, but collectively thinkable." This is Philo's expression. In the *Timæus* of Plato, the words are almost identical with the Bible ones, "Now when the Father, who had created the universe, saw how it had become living and animated, and an image of the eternal gods, he felt pleasure therein." In the Bible we read, "And God saw that it was good."

The recognition of the divine is for Philo, as well as for Plato and in the wisdom of the Mysteries, to live through the process of creation in one's own soul. The history of creation and the history of the soul which is becoming divine, in this way flow into one. Philo is convinced that Moses' account of the creation may be used for writing the history of the soul which is seeking God. Everything in the Bible thereby acquires a profoundly symbolical meaning, of which Philo becomes the interpreter. He reads the Bible as a history of the soul.

We may say that Philo's manner of reading the Bible corresponds to a feature of his age which originated in the wisdom of the Mysteries. He indeed relates that the Therapeutæ interpreted ancient writings in the same way. "They also possess works by ancient authors who once directed their school and left behind many explanations about the customary method pursued in allegorical writings.... The interpretation of such writings is directed to the deeper meaning of the allegorical narratives" (*cf.* p. 200). Thus Philo's aim was to discover the deeper meaning of the "allegorical" narratives in the Old Testament.

Let us try to realise whither such an interpretation could lead. We read the account of creation and find in it not only a narrative of outward events, but an indication of the way which the soul has to take in order to attain to the divine. Thus the soul must reproduce in itself, as a microcosm, the ways of God, and in this alone can its efforts after wisdom consist. The drama of the universe must be enacted in each individual soul. The inner life of the mystical sage is the realisation of the image given in the account of creation. Moses wrote not only to relate historical facts, but to represent pictorially the paths which the soul must travel if it would find God.

All this, in Philo's conception of the universe, is enacted within the human soul. Man experiences within himself what God has experienced in the universe. The word of God, the Logos, becomes an event in the soul. God brought the Jews from Egypt into Palestine; he let them go through distress and privation before giving them that Land of Promise. That is the outward event. Man must experience it inwardly. He goes from the land of Egypt, the perishable world, through the privations which lead to the suppression of the sense-nature, into the Promised Land of the soul, he attains the eternal. With Philo it is all an inward process. The God who poured Himself forth into the world consummates His resurrection in the soul when that soul understands His creative word and echoes it. Then man has spiritually given birth within himself to divinity, to the divine spirit which became man, to the Logos, Christ. In this sense knowledge was, for Philo and those who thought like him, the birth of Christ within the world of spirit. The Neo-Platonic philosophy, which developed contemporaneously with Christianity, was an elaboration of Philo's thought. Let us see how Plotinus (A.D. 204-269) describes his spiritual experiences:

"Often when I come to myself on awaking from bodily sleep and, turning from the outer world, enter into myself, I behold wondrous beauty. Then I am sure that I have been conscious of the better part of myself. I live my true life, I am one with the divine and, rooted in the divine, gain the power to transport myself beyond even the super-world. After thus resting in God, when I descend from spiritual vision and again form thoughts, I ask myself how it has happened that I now descend and that my soul ever entered the body at all, since, in its essence, it is what it has just revealed itself to me. What can the reason be for souls forgetting God the Father since they come from the beyond and belong to Him, and, when they forget Him, know nothing of Him or of themselves? The first false step they take is indulging in presumption, the desire to become, and in forgetfulness of their true self and in the pleasure of only belonging to themselves. They coveted self-glorification, they rushed about in pursuit of their desires and thus went astray and fell completely away. Thereupon they lost all knowledge of their origin in the beyond, just as children, early separated from their parents and brought up elsewhere, do not know who they themselves and their parents are." Plotinus delineates the kind of life which the soul should strive to develop. "The life of the body and its longings should be stilled, the soul should see calm in all that surrounds it: in earth, sea, air, and heaven itself no movement. It should learn to see how the soul pours itself from without into the serene cosmos, streaming into it from all sides; as the sun's rays illuminate a dark cloud and make it golden, so does the soul, on entering the body of the world encircled by the sky, give it life and immortality."

It is evident that this vision of the world is very similar to that of Christianity. Believers of the community of Jesus said: "That which was from the beginning, which we have heard, which we have seen with our eyes, which we have looked upon, and our hands have handled, of the Word of life ... declare we unto you." In the same way it might be said in the spirit of Neo-Platonism, "That which was from the beginning, which cannot be heard and seen, must be spiritually experienced as the Word of life."

And so the old conception of the universe is developed and splits into two leading ideas. It leads in Neo-Platonism and similar systems to an idea of Christ which is purely spiritual; on the other hand, it leads to a fusion of the idea of Christ with a historical manifestation, the personality of Jesus. The writer of the Gospel of St. John may be said to unite these two conceptions. "In the beginning was the Word." He shares this conviction with the Neo-Platonists. The Word becomes spirit within the soul, thus do the Neo-Platonists conclude. The Word was made flesh in Jesus, thus does St. John conclude, and with him the whole Christian community. The inner meaning of the manner in which the Word was made flesh was given in all the ancient cosmogonies. Plato says of the macrocosm: "God has extended the body of the world on the soul of the world in the form of a cross." The soul of the world is the Logos. If the Logos is to be made flesh, he must recapitulate the cosmic process in fleshly existence. He must be nailed to the cross, and rise again. In spiritual form this most momentous thought of Christianity had long before been prefigured in the old cosmogonies. The Mystic went through it as a personal experience in initiation. The Logos become man had to go through it in a way that made this fact one that is true for or valid to the whole of humanity. Something which was present under the old dispensation as an incident in the Mysteries becomes a historical fact through Christianity. Hence Christianity was the fulfilment not only of what the Jewish prophets had predicted, but also of the truth which had been prefigured in the Mysteries.

The Cross of Golgotha gathers together in one fact the whole cult of the Mysteries of antiquity. We find the cross first in the ancient cosmogonies. At the starting-point of Christianity it confronts us in an unique event which has supreme value for the whole of mankind. It is from this point of view that it is possible for the reason to apprehend the mystical element in Christianity. Christianity as a mystical fact is a milestone in the process of human evolution; and the incidents in the Mysteries, with their attendant results, are the preparation for that mystical fact.

XIII

ST. AUGUSTINE AND THE CHURCH

The full force of the conflict which was enacted in the souls of Christian believers during the transition from paganism to the new religion is exhibited in the person of St. Augustine (A.D. 354-430). The spiritual struggles of Origen, Clement of Alexandria, Gregory Nazianzen, Jerome, and others are full of mysterious interest when we see them calmed and laid to rest in the mind of Augustine.

In Augustine's personality deep spiritual needs developed out of a passionate nature. He passed through pagan and semi-Christian ideas. He suffered deeply from the most appalling doubts of the land which attack one who has felt the impotence of many varieties of thought in the face of spiritual problems, and who has tasted the depressing effect of the question: "Can man know anything whatever?"

At the beginning of his struggles, Augustine's thoughts clung to the perishable things of sense. He could only picture the spiritual to himself in material images. It is a deliverance for him when he rises above this stage. He thus describes it in his *Confessions*: "When I wished to think of God, I could only imagine immense masses of bodies and believed that was the only kind of thing that could exist. This was the chief and almost the only cause of the errors which I could not avoid." He thus indicates the point at which a person must arrive who is seeking the true life of the spirit. There are thinkers, not a few, who maintain that it is impossible to arrive at pure thought, free from any material admixture. These thinkers confuse what they feel bound to say about their own inner life, with what is humanly possible. The truth rather is that it is only possible to arrive at higher knowledge when thought has been liberated from all material things, when an inner life has been developed in which images of reality do not cease when their demonstration in sense-impressions comes to an end. Augustine relates how he attained to spiritual vision. Everywhere he asked where the divine was to be found. "I asked the earth and she said 'I am not it' and all that was upon the earth said the same. I asked the ocean and the abysses and all that lives in them, which said, 'We are not thy God, seek beyond us.' I asked the winds, and the whole atmosphere and its inhabitants said, 'The philosophers who sought for the essence of things in us were under an illusion, we are not God.' I asked the sun, moon, and stars, which said, 'We are not God whom thou seekest.'" And it came home to St. Augustine that there is only one thing which can answer his question about the divine—his own soul. The soul said, "No eyes nor ears can impart to thee what is in me. For I alone can tell thee, and I tell thee in an unquestionable way." "Men may be doubtful whether vital force is situate in air or in fire, but who can doubt that he himself lives, remembers, understands, wills, thinks, knows, and judges? If he doubts, it is a proof that he is alive, he remembers why he doubts, he understands that he doubts, he will assure himself of things, he thinks, he knows that he knows nothing, he judges that he must not accept anything hastily." Outer things do not defend themselves when their essence and existence are denied, but the soul does defend itself. It could not be doubtful of itself unless it existed. By its doubt it confirms its own existence. "We are and we recognise our being, and we love our own being and knowledge. On these three points no illusion in the garb of truth can trouble us, for we do not apprehend them with our bodily senses like external things." Man learns about the divine by leading his soul to know itself as spiritual, so that it may find its way, as a spirit, into the spiritual world. Augustine had battled his way through to this knowledge. It was out of such an attitude of mind that there grew up in pagan nations the desire to knock at the gate of the Mysteries. In the age of Augustine, such convictions might lead to becoming a Christian. Jesus, the Logos become man had shown the path which must be followed by the soul if it would attain the goal which it sees when in communion with itself. In A.D. 385, at Milan, Augustine was instructed by St. Ambrose. All his doubts about the Old and New Testaments vanished when his teacher interpreted the most important passages, not merely in a literal sense, but "by lifting the mystic veil by force of the spirit."

What had been guarded in the Mysteries was embodied for Augustine in the historical tradition of the Evangelists and in the community where that tradition was preserved. He comes by degrees to the conviction that "the law of this tradition, which consists in believing what it has not proved, is moderate and without guile." He arrives at the idea, "Who could be so blind as to say that the Church of the Apostles deserves to have no faith placed in it, when it is so loyal and is supported by the conformity of so many brethren; when these have handed down their writings to posterity so conscientiously, and when the Church has so strictly maintained the succession of teachers, down to our present bishops?"

Augustine's mode of thought told him, that with the coming of Christ other conditions had set in for souls seeking after the spirit than those which had previously existed. For him it was firmly established that in Christ Jesus had been revealed in outer historical fact that which the Mystic had sought in the Mysteries through preparation. One of his most significant utterances is the following, "What is now called the Christian religion already existed amongst the ancients and was not lacking at the very beginnings of the human race. When Christ appeared in the flesh, the true religion already in existence received the name of Christian." There were two ways possible for such a method of thought. One way is that if the human soul develops within it the forces which lead it to the knowledge of its true self, it will, if it only goes far enough, come also to the knowledge of the Christ and of everything connected with him. This would have been a mystery-wisdom enriched through the Christ event. The other way is taken by Augustine and is that by which he became the great model for his successors. It consists in cutting off the development of the forces of the soul at a certain point, and in borrowing the ideas connected with the coming of Christ from written accounts and oral traditions. Augustine rejected the first way as springing from pride of the soul; he thought the second was the way of true humility. Thus he says to those who wished to follow the first way: "You may find peace in the truth, but for that humility is needed, which does not suit your proud neck." On the other hand, he was filled with boundless inward happiness by the fact that since the coming of Christ in the flesh, it was possible to say that every soul can come to spiritual experience which goes as far as it can in seeking within itself, and then, in order to attain to the highest, has confidence in what the written and oral traditions of the Christian Church tell us about the Christ and his revelation. He says on this point: "What bliss, what abiding enjoyment of supreme and true good is offered us, what serenity, what a breath of eternity! How shall I describe it? It has been expressed, as far as it could be, by those great incomparable souls who we admit have beheld and still behold.... We reach a point at which we acknowledge how true is what we have been commanded to believe and how well and beneficently we have been brought up by our mother, the Church, and of what benefit was the milk given by the Apostle Paul to the little ones...." (It is beyond the scope of this book to give an account of the alternative method which is evolved from the Mystery Wisdom, enriched through the Christ event. The description of this method will be found in *An Outline of Occult Science*, see advt., front page.) Whereas in pre-Christian times one who wished to seek the spiritual basis of existence was necessarily directed to the way of the Mysteries, Augustine was able to say, even to those souls who could find no such path within themselves, "Go as far as you can on the path of knowledge with your human powers, thence trust (faith) will carry you up into the higher spiritual regions." It was only going one step further to say, it is natural to the human soul only to be able to arrive at a certain stage of knowledge through its own powers: thence it can only advance further through trust, through faith in written and oral tradition. This step was taken by the spiritual movement which assigned to knowledge a certain sphere above which the soul could not rise by its own efforts, but everything which lay beyond this domain was made an object of faith which has to be supported by written and oral tradition and by confidence in its representatives. Thomas Aquinas, the greatest teacher within the Church (1224-1274), has set forth this doctrine in his writings in a variety of ways. His main point is that human knowledge can only attain to that which led Augustine to self-knowledge, to the certainty of the divine. The nature of the divine and its relation to the world is given by revealed theology, which is not accessible to man's own researches and is, as the substance of faith, superior to all knowledge.

The origin of this point of view may be studied in the theology of John Scotus Erigena, who lived in the ninth century at the court of Charles the Bald, and who represents a natural transition from the earliest ideas of Christianity to the ideas of Thomas Aquinas. His conception of the universe is couched in the spirit of Neo-Platonism. In his treatise *De Divisione Naturæ*, Erigena has elaborated the teaching of Dionysius the Areopagite. This teaching started from a God far above the perishable things of sense, and it derived the world from Him (*Cf.* p. 208 *et seq.*). Man is involved in the transmutation of all beings into this God, Who finally becomes what He was from the beginning. Everything falls back again into the Godhead which has passed through the universal process and has finally become perfected. But in order to reach this goal man must find the way to the Logos who was made flesh. In Erigena this thought leads to another: that what is contained in the writings which give an account of the Logos leads, when received in faith, to salvation. Reason and the authority of the Scriptures, faith and knowledge stand on the same level. The one does not contradict the other, but faith must bring that to which knowledge never can attain by itself.

The knowledge of the eternal which the ancient Mysteries withheld from the multitude became, when presented in this way by Christian thought and feeling, the content of faith, which by its very nature had to do with something unattainable by mere knowledge. The conviction of the pre-Christian Mystic was that to him was given knowledge of the divine, while the people were obliged to have faith in its expression in images. Christianity came to the conviction that God has given his wisdom to mankind through revelation, and man attains through his knowledge an image of this divine revelation. The wisdom of the Mysteries is a hothouse plant, which is revealed to a few individuals ripe for it. Christian wisdom is a Mystery revealed as knowledge to none, but as a content of faith revealed to all. The standpoint of the Mysteries lived on in Christianity, but in a different form. All, not only the special individual, were to share in the truth, but the process was that at a certain point man owned his inability to penetrate farther by means of knowledge, and thence ascended to faith. Christianity brought the content of the Mysteries out of the obscurity of the temple into the clear light of day. The one Christian movement mentioned led to the idea that this content must necessarily be retained in the form of faith.

NOTES

P. 5—To one who has true perception, the "Spirit of Nature" speaks powerfully in the facts currently expressed by the catchword, "struggle for existence," etc.; but not in the opinions which modern science deduces from them. In the first statement lies the reason why natural science is attracting more and more widespread attention. But it follows from the second statement that scientific opinions should not be taken as if they necessarily belonged to a knowledge of facts. The possibility of being led astray by mere opinion is, in these days, infinitely great.

P. 9—It should not be concluded from these remarks about the sources of St. Luke's Gospel, that purely historical research is undervalued by the writer of this book. This is not the case. Historical research is absolutely justified, but it should not be impatient with the method of presentation proceeding from a spiritual point of view. It is not considered of importance to make various kinds of quotations in this book; but one who is willing will be able to see that a really unprejudiced, broad-minded judgment will not find anything that is here stated to be contrary to what has been actually and historically proved. One who will not be broad-minded, but who holds this or that theory to be a firmly-established fact, may easily think that assertions made in this book are untenable from a scientific point of view, and are made without any objective foundation.

P. 15—It is said above that those whose spiritual eyes are opened are able to see into the spiritual world. The conclusion must not on this account be drawn that only one who possesses spiritual sight is able to form an intelligent opinion about the results arrived at by the initiate. Spiritual sight belongs only to the investigator. If he afterwards communicates what he has discovered, every one can understand it who gives fair play to his reason and preserves an unbiassed sense of truth. And such an one may also apply the results of research to life and derive satisfaction from them without himself having spiritual sight.

P. 20—"The sinking into the mire" spoken of by Plato must also be interpreted in the sense referred to in the last note.

P. 20—What is said about the impossibility of imparting the teaching of the Mysteries has reference to the fact that they could not be communicated to those unprepared in the same form in which the initiate experienced them; but they were always communicated to those outside in such a form as was possible for the uninitiated to understand. For instance the myths gave the old form, in order to communicate the content of the Mysteries in a way that was generally comprehensible.

P. 88—Everything that relates to knowledge gained through the "eyes of the spirit" is called by ancient mysticism "Mantik." "Telestik," on the other hand, is the indication of the ways which lead to initiation.

P. 168—"Kabirs," according to ancient mysticism, are beings with a consciousness far above the human consciousness of to-day. Schelling means that man through initiation ascends to a state of consciousness above his present one.

P. 186—An explanation of the meaning of the number seven may be obtained in *An Outline of Occult Science* (see advt., front page).

P. 187—The meanings of the Apocalyptic signs can only be given quite shortly here. Of course, all these things might be much more thoroughly explained, but of this the scope of this book does not allow.

THE END

www.ingramcontent.com/pod-product-compliance
Ingram Content Group UK Ltd.
Pitfield, Milton Keynes, MK11 3LW, UK
UKHW040820280325
456847UK00003B/560